In the Footsteps of the

East London Group

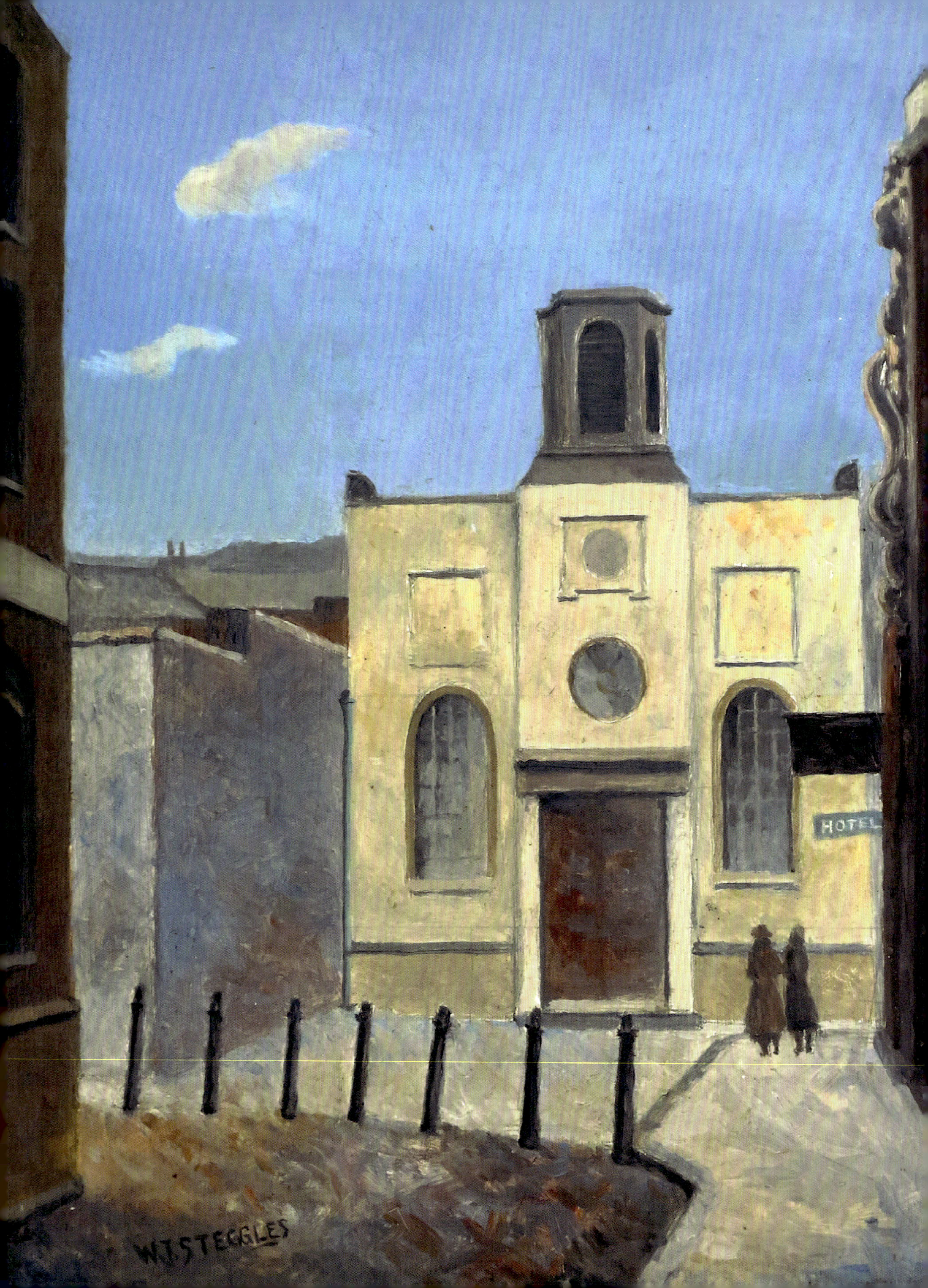
HOTEL
W.J.STEGGLES

In the Footsteps of the East London Group

Reflections on the works of the East London Group by painters of the contemporary urban landscape

Alan Waltham, Ferha Farooqui,
Frank Creber and the Nunnery Gallery

BATSFORD

Front cover image: *Lost in Spitalfields*, Doreen Fletcher (2024)
Back cover image: *Blue Bridge, Wilton Way, Hackney*, James Mackinnon (2024)

Previous page: *The Chapel*, Walter Steggles (1932)
At first glance, this painting has a decidedly Mediterranean feel to it. However, the location is the Church of Holy Trinity, Minories. Very sadly, the chapel was destroyed by bombing during World War II, but the pulpit, which was removed in 1906 after the church was closed, can still be seen in All Saints' Church in East Meon.

First published in the United Kingdom in 2024 by
Batsford
43 Great Ormond Street
London
WC1N 3HZ

An imprint of B. T. Batsford Holdings Limited

ISBN 978 1 84994 935 4

A CIP catalogue record for this book is available from the British Library.

10 9 8 7 6 5 4 3 2 1

Reproduction by Rival Colour Ltd, UK
Printed and bound by Elma Basim, Turkey

This book can be ordered direct from the publisher at www.batsfordbooks.com, or try your local bookshop.

MIX
Paper from responsible sources
FSC® C164814

Contents

Foreword

by Sophie Hill, the Nunnery Gallery

It is said that there is a higher concentration of artists in East London than in any other city in Europe. Artists have made, and continue to make, East London one of the most creative and culturally diverse areas of the city, and the East London Group (ELG) is an integral thread in this history.

Bow Arts has been supporting East London's artist community for thirty years, providing affordable studios and a free public exhibition space at the Nunnery Gallery. The gallery programme explores the stories of East London, and we were proud to exhibit one of the first retrospectives of the East London Group back in 2014. As an organization with a growing and thriving artist community, celebrating today's artistic talent is incredibly important, so to bring together paintings from both East London's past and its present feels very meaningful indeed.

The East London Group continually captivates our audience's imagination, as they lived, worked and painted on the streets surrounding the gallery. Breaking the mould of a patronized or wealthy artist, many painted alongside their day jobs – window cleaner, basket weaver, errand boy – making art when they could and where they could, as many of our artists still do today. They painted the streets, buildings and corners of East London as it was the area that surrounded them, capturing fleeting and much-loved scenes, many of which have since changed or disappeared and might otherwise have been forgotten.

Their work consistently found beauty in areas that traditionally would not have been painted: a timber yard, railway arches, or what were then industrial backwaters. This love of locality and the ability to capture the essence of the East End is what transcends time in these pictures, summoning lines, shadows and light that convey such personal reminiscence, yet appeal to so many. This recognizability of streets that are familiar yet were painted years ago bewitches our audiences each time we exhibit these paintings.

Showing these historical works alongside contemporary interpretations of the same, or similarly inspired, scenes is a very special exploration. Not only is it an exercise in 'then' and 'now', but also a celebration of the artist's perspective in bringing a place alive, by igniting seemingly mundane bricks and mortar with memory and experience. As the East London Group artists enabled their streets to sing, so do the artists of the Urban Contemporaries Group, filling scenes with emotion, stories and the communities that thrive within them.

In a city that is changing perhaps faster than ever before, the Urban Contemporaries and invited artists are also consciously immortalizing scenes and buildings that may very well disappear. Even the streets that surround the Nunnery Gallery look very different to those we moved into nearly thirty years ago. It is with double intrigue that visitors will peer into these paintings, exploring the East London of the 1920s and 30s – wondering at the quiet street in Grace Oscroft's *Old Houses, Bow* (page 77), which today has the Bow flyover and A12 thundering past – but also pausing to reflect on how East London is changing today, as Harriet Mena Hill remembers the recently demolished *Clarissa House (Poplar)* (page 88). Both sites shown in these pictures are a short walk from the gallery.

This will be the third exhibition that the Nunnery Gallery has hosted showcasing the East London Group paintings, together with exhibitions that have explored the streets and scenes of East London – our retrospective of Doreen Fletcher, who also shows work in this exhibition, being a notable one. These exhibitions have been some of our best attended. Locals who have long since moved out of East London travel back to reminisce in their streets. Newcomers marvel at the rich history and hidden corners that their new local area encompasses. Visitors of all ages are fascinated by how their city has changed and how it has not; how many little details have stayed the same, and how other scenes are barely recognizable. Either way, these are the houses and streets that have borne witness to the people passing across the ages, and they have each been immortalized by the emotive flourish of the artist's brush.

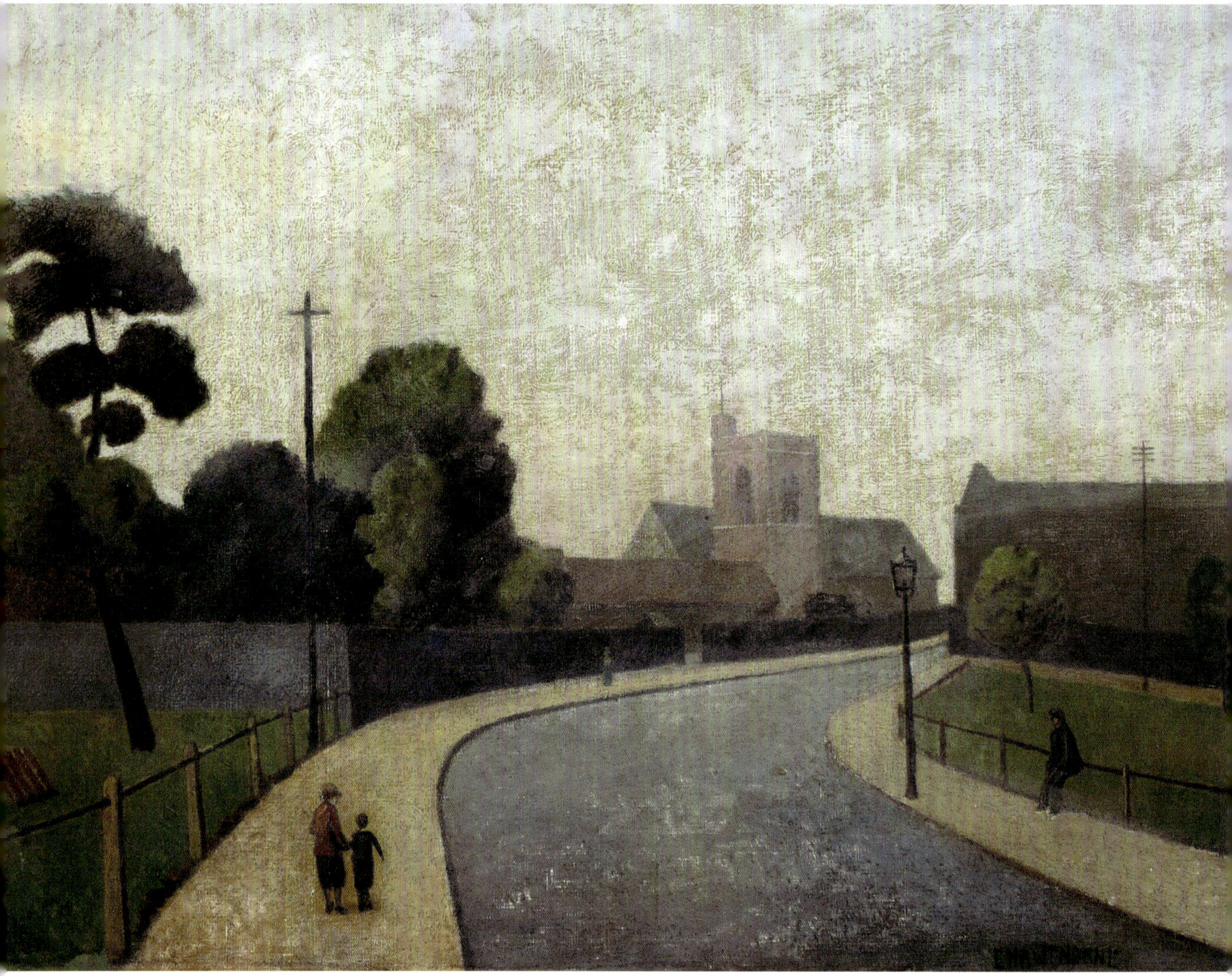

Eastern Avenue, E15, Elwin Hawthorne (1932)

Sold from exhibition in 1932, this painting subsequently appeared in a shop in Southwold some years ago. Elwin's painting notes describe it as follows: 'From Temple Mills Lane End. Church in distance: trees on left. Man sitting on fence. Two children in foreground. From near dog racing track.'

Introduction

by Ferha Farooqui and Frank Creber,
curators of the Urban Contemporaries Group

The artist/curator-led journey for this exhibition commenced in summer 2022, when we first approached Alan Waltham, curator of a magnificent collection of original paintings by the East London Group (ELG). Our intention was to open a window to this group of early twentieth-century artists, as well as to the past life of East London, and an earlier time in British art, to juxtapose their paintings with works created by contemporary artists interested in reflecting upon the modern urban landscape.

Our brief was simple. We aimed to bring together around thirty-five original paintings by members of the East London Group and show them alongside twenty-two contemporary interpretations of the locations and themes that absorbed this earlier generation of British artists around the environments of Bow. Our geographical 'footprint' echoed that of the ELG and extended west as far as Canonbury (Islington), Bethnal Green and Spitalfields, and east to Stratford, including what is now the Olympic Park and surrounding areas.

The Nunnery Gallery's programme pushes boundaries in exploring the stories of East London. Its vision, and its location in the pivotal centre of Bow, was a happy and wonderful happenstance, while the gallery's previous support for two extraordinary and successful shows about the East London Group meant that we received their ready and generous support in bringing together the works of this early generation of painters to enable new audiences to examine their canvases next to contemporary artists working in the urban landscape tradition now.

The mainly working-class men and women artists of the ELG studied at the Bethnal Green Working Men's Institute. They were taught by some of the leading British modernist artists of their day, and were encouraged to explore their urban environment to develop a visual language that celebrated the beauty of the everyday.

We chose the contemporary artists involved in this exhibition because of their passion for creating work that responds to the urban condition. Each contemporary artist brought with them very personal encounters with the locations that inspired the East London Group of artists. Some were based on direct observations of the localities that inspired some of the ELG, whereas others offered social and biographical reflection – there have been myriad interpretations of the theme. Each contemporary artist chosen to be part of our venture brought with them a deep respect and curiosity for the history of East London, and for these paintings from a hundred years ago made on the streets of Bow and beyond by earlier artists who brought their innovative observations to everyday scenes of Britain in the first half of the twentieth century.

The medium of painting was significant because the Urban Contemporaries Group promotes painting as a unique form of engagement with the subject. The expressive quality of this medium enables a rendition, over time, of the subjectivity of the individual artist, shaped by their personal feelings and observations.

The curators' aim has also been to offer a diversity of 'voices' by inviting an even mix of male and female artists from established, mid-career and early-career backgrounds, to ensure that different perspectives were conveyed. We were extraordinarily gratified that almost all the artists created new paintings specifically for this show, while others enthusiastically lent themselves to our endeavours by offering paintings that resonated strongly with the theme.

We are endlessly grateful to Alan Waltham for bringing together around thirty-five original paintings by the East London Group from collections around the country – a formidable task! We have been delighted to be offered the wonderful chance to capture this exhibition in a dedicated book of the show by Polly Powell of Batsford Books, who is the granddaughter of John Cooper and Phyllis Bray, members and champions of the East London Group.

The curators have been astounded by the enthusiasm with which this exhibition idea has been embraced by each artist. Each has also offered their own written reflections on their very individual approach, which the reader can enjoy later in the book.

We were delighted to be joined by **David Hepher** on this project. By happy coincidence, his magnificent painting *North Face I* (page 31), about the former Robin Hood Gardens in Poplar, was just being completed when we approached him with the idea for our show, which captured his imagination. Robin Hood Gardens is a nationally important and internationally recognized work of Brutalist architecture. Completed in 1972, the building was designed by Alison and Peter Smithson, British architects of international reputation. It has now been largely demolished as part of the redevelopment of the area. Our introduction of the East London Group to David stimulated a wonderful written response that captures the 'disappearance' from contemporary art history of these predominantly working-class artists of an earlier age.

It was gratifying to receive the support and involvement of **Doreen Fletcher**, an artist who is interested in the 'pockets of life others ignore'. She paints East London and is constantly drawn to the dichotomy of change and permanence encapsulated in the one subject. Her painting

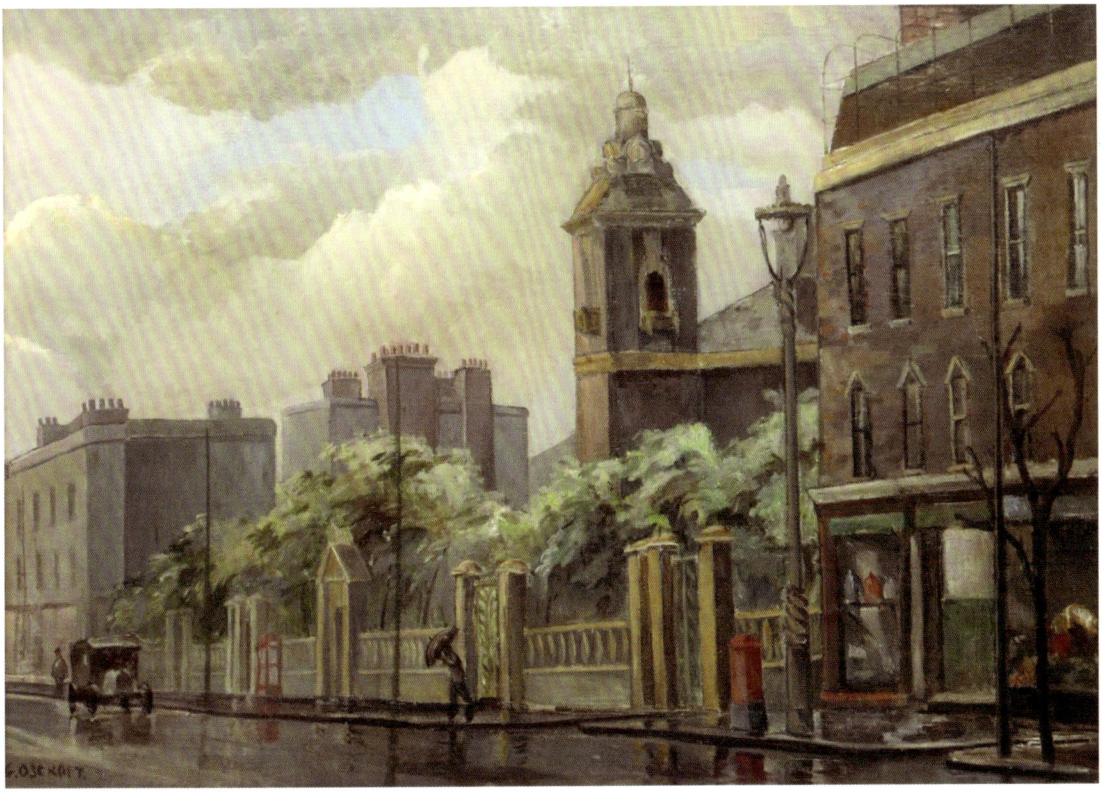

St Clement's Hospital, Grace Oscroft (undated)

Starting life as the City of London Union Workhouse in 1849, the building became the City of London Union Infirmary in 1874 and, after various name changes, thereafter became a psychiatric unit in 1936. It was known as St Clement's Hospital until its closure in 2006. It then became London's first development under the Community Land Trust in 2012, with work starting on the site in 2014.

Lost in Spitalfields (page 34) reflects on a location near Petticoat Lane in the back streets away from the 'trendier' Spitalfields Market; it is a location that would have attracted members of the ELG.

Timothy Hyman's very personal encounter with Canonbury Tower (Islington), a Tudor landmark amid nineteenth-century terraces, is reflected in his painting *Under Canonbury Tower* (page 81). This is a tender, autobiographical portrait of a much-loved symbol of the artist's engagement with East London and reflects on a recent personal loss, incorporating symbolic elements such as Saturn and reflecting emotions tied to his identity and experience.

Michael Johnson's *Cambridge Heath Road* (page 52) also offers a very individual encounter with London and resonates with his poetic and lyrical impressions of the East End of the capital. Sketching from buses, he captured fleeting scenes while interacting with fellow passengers. The area's historical depth, from ancient train lines to rewilded landscapes, resonates with Johnson's enduring connection to East London's maritime and industrial heritage.

Ben Johnson's fascinating painting *Moving East* (page 38) celebrates the connection between institutions that fostered the invention, ambition and creativity of working-class East London artists and craftspeople from the time of the East London Group, and the continuation of this ambition today with the movement eastward of the Victoria and Albert Museum (V&A), first to the former Bethnal Green Museum of Childhood (now the Young V&A) and now to the forthcoming O'Donnell + Tuomey's new V&A East, in the Queen Elizabeth Olympic Park. This work references the influence of the 1851 Great Exhibition at the Crystal Palace and its legacy as the V&A. The move of the V&A to Stratford echoes the East London Group's journey from Bethnal Green, highlighting their connection to the area's inventive spirit.

We have been very gratified to discover that many of the artists involved have embraced the theme as part of their individual artistic practice. For example, **Grant Watson** produced *Trinity Green Chapel* (page 55) at the end of a year-long journey that involved creating a three-dimensional model of the Trinity Almshouses, Mile End Road, depicted by ELG member Elwin Hawthorne. From this, more than twenty paintings and drawings emerged, creating conversations between painting and model. A few of these works now no longer exist, painted over, changed or transformed. The artist says of his approach: 'the whole process was like a tennis player practising a serve over and over again'; the result is a sort of magic.

Alexandra Blum usually creates lyrical monochrome drawings, so it was captivating to witness her embrace of colourful, painterly mark-making in *West India Dock (boundary between here and there)* (page 62). Here, she explored the rhythm and life of contemporary Docklands and offered a visually fascinating vision of the modern city, inspired by Walter Steggles' *Freighters in West India Dock*. Drawing at the dock, Blum found bustling activity replacing past desolation. Blum's painting captures dynamic layers and unfolding events, revealing the dock's historical context from colonial exploitation to contemporary urban life. Her art reflects detailed observations of spatial rhythms and interactions.

Fiona McIntyre's *Bow Back Rivers Algae Bloom* (page 64) reflects on contemporary concerns about the pollution of our waterways and aquatic life. The artist spent time painting many sketches of the waterways around Bow Back River to capture several versions of this almost fluorescent algae-bloomed stretch of the river in summer 2023, before alighting on a very subtle vision of East London's connection to similar concerns of the past.

Hilary Rosen's triptych *Bethnal Green and East India Docklands* (page 72) reflects her childhood in the area. Inspired by urban scenes such as Albert Turpin's *The Arches, Cambridge Heath Road*, she delivers a wonderful watercolour piece. Her work also draws from Walter Steggles' *Freighters in West India Dock*, capturing old and modern architectural contrasts. The triptych symbolizes East London's connectivity and Rosen's passion for urban art.

Tim Craven's fascinating painting process has taken years to develop. His approach involves a unique method of focusing on individual sections sequentially, creating a mysterious yet deliberate visual narrative. He says of his work *Regent's Canal (Grove Road)* (page 82): 'I only see the section (and painting) I am working on, and when happy it's finished, it is covered up and I move on to the next one in bands so that there are no distractions. Each new section is another universe to get to know. I don't know what it will really look like as a whole, and over four months I can't remember past sections. It is an unconventional process, and I have always been drawn to unconventional ways of painting. Sequencing is key to everything – light into dark or dark into light. In fact, it's both, but a cerebral puzzle every time.'

Afternoon Light, Antill Road by **Marc Gooderham** (page 84) beautifully captures a moment in the ever-changing landscape of London's East End. It documents the passage of time in this vibrant and evolving community – a goal the artist has always set out to achieve. His work reflects on the essence of East London, resonating with the East London Group's ethos of capturing everyday beauty. Inspired by Elwin Hawthorne's work, Gooderham sketches vibrant street scenes such as Mile End Road. His connection to the group is profound, influenced by their documentation of the East End's evolution.

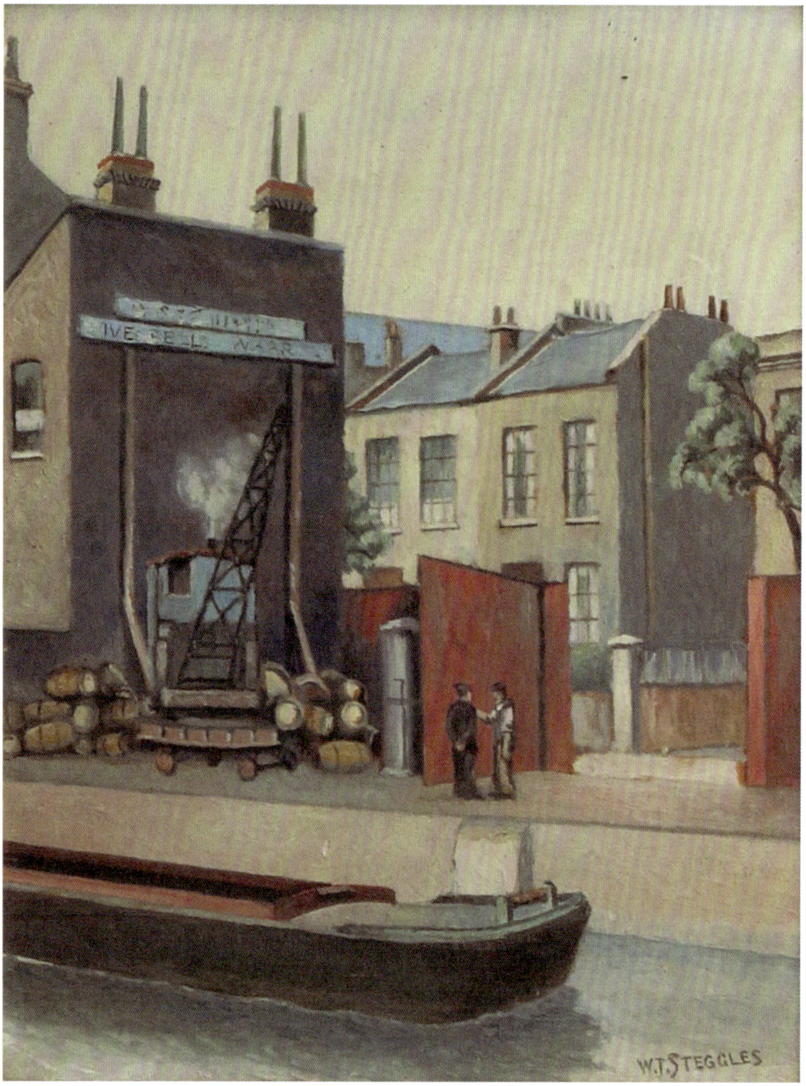

Five Bells Wharf, Walter Steggles (1931)

This was a view from the footbridge that crossed the Lea Navigation near the old Bryant and May factory. The wharf was next door to the Five Bells Wharf public house at 535 Old Ford Road. The bridge itself features in Walter's painting *Red Bridge* and was also his viewpoint for *Canal at Bow* that dates from 1931.

James Mackinnon's *Blue Bridge, Wilton Way, Hackney* (page 94) reveals the artist's preoccupation with a scene, the original inspiration for which may have been John Minton's painting *Street and Railway Bridge*. It is an attempt to focus the viewer's gaze onto a very ordinary but beautiful structure, sitting quietly and unnoticed on 'an unremarkable working day, far removed from Minton's bridge, which inhabited the dramatic scene of a bomb-damaged London street'.

The vanishing of parts of East London is felt in the paintings and observations of Doreen Fletcher, Philippa Beale, Harriet Mena Hill, Ferha Farooqui, Annette Fernando and the young graduate artist, Nicole Poh.

Philippa Beale's *After Harold Steggles, Memories St Mark's Church and Mare Street* (page 69) movingly reflects on the loss of East London's previous connections to education and industry, alongside exploring her own and her family's direct connections to the area through her teaching work and her husband's former family business in the area. She explores her East End memories, which have been affected by urban change, and emphasizes nature's resilience amid societal shifts, which often erase community heritage. Churches such as St Mark's inspire her paintings, recalling vanished views from the East London Group era.

Harriet Mena Hill's *Clarissa House (Poplar)* (page 88) fascinatingly uses salvaged material to provide a link with a former 'unknowable history and purpose'. Her work involves collecting substrates, which she lives with in her studio for months or sometimes years, getting to know their shape and feel, waiting to find the image that will inhabit the surface and ultimately give them a new life – 'finding value in the discarded'. Her intention was to salvage material from the proximity of Clarissa House where the building was located, but when she returned to the site the building had been demolished and the ground cleared. Her final panel was sourced from Canning Town, another area of East London undergoing significant transformation.

Ferha Farooqui's *Lost Highway* (page 44) captures the evolving landscape of Stratford, East London, blending past and present in a visual 'timescape'. The luminous blues symbolize the remains and signs of the past, including rediscovered elements such as the vanished Harrow public house and cottages. Blue figures represent former inhabitants mingling with today's population, echoing the work of Walter Steggles. Farooqui's art reflects urban drama and lost histories, bridging generations of East London's streets.

Annette Fernando's work *Sparrows Can't Sing* (page 86) delves into East London's vanished history through archival research, inspired by the 1963 film *Sparrows Can't Sing*. Her work captures the emotional impact of urban renewal, symbolized by Balfron Tower, using a film motif to reflect cycles of demolition and reconstruction and evoking introspection on change and loss.

Tower – Bryant and May Building by **Gethin Evans** (page 91) demonstrates the artist's captivation by the water tower of the old Bryant and May building located near his studio. Inspired by Ambrogio Lorenzetti's art and the match girls' strike history, he depicted the tower as a witness to past injustices. His painting captures the mood before a storm, echoing historical narratives. It is a testimony to the conditions of former workers and a powerful form of bearing witness to the past.

It was wonderful to discover the work of **Nicole Poh** at Camberwell Art College's BA Graduate Show of 2023. We asked Nicole to join our show, and she arrived at a painting entitled *Austerity, Dehumanisation, Disappearance* (page 75) that powerfully encapsulates the loss of 'contentious' architecture from the East London landscape. She was also captivated by the Robin Hood Gardens: her painting investigates the impact on society of the materials utilized in these buildings, which would perhaps be better preserved in other parts of London, but sadly face a grim reckoning in East London.

Frank Creber's enigmatic painting for this show, *The Limping Man Clue* (page 40), is a response to the ninety years that connect the world of the East London Group of artists and the perhaps not so dissimilar contemporary concerns of today. It features the Guardian Angels Church in Mile End, inspired by Elwin Hawthorne's work. It offers a narrative that stems from a 1939 newspaper article about a theft of cigarettes, connecting past experiences of East London with Creber's personal experiences of working with local families. Creber's work is informed by forty years' experience as an artist, developing practical projects with local families in art and well-being, social enterprise, the environment and community arts, at the Bromley by Bow Centre in East London.

Sarah Lowe's painting *Wicked* (page 48) is inspired by Walter Steggles' *Stratford*. It reflects on the transient nature of cities, the human connection and the beauty of ordinary landscapes impacted by those who inhabit them.

Melissa Scott-Miller always works from life in the urban landscape. She carefully captures the rich detail of the city, from its detritus to its houses, churches, trees and community gardens. Her painting *View of Canonbury Tower, Summer 2023* (page 78) records her painstaking personal encounter with the same subject matter that so thoroughly captivated Harold Steggles in 1938.

Alex Pemberton has painted visions of the Thames and the urban landscapes it traverses for most of his life. Inspired by Walter Steggles' painting *Freighters in West India Dock*, his painting *Tate* *and Lyle Factory, Silvertown* (page 59) takes as its focal point a building that has been a significant East End landmark since 1878. Pemberton captures the factory's scale by focusing on sections of its facade, revealing a human history through its architecture and eccentric details. The painting's angular forms and layered composition resemble a frieze, depicting depth and structure in a flat frontal plane.

As curators, we have enjoyed working closely with the artists, understanding their processes and witnessing the passion they bring to their work. We have been deeply committed to nurturing the artistic vision of each participant in this exhibition and fostering a collaborative environment. Each artist's exploration of themes such as community identity, historical preservation and the changing urban landscape has enriched our experience and deepened our appreciation for East End London's enduring spirit.

This exhibition showcases the diverse themes and methods among the participating artists. They explore urban change and community heritage, emphasizing nature's resilience. Historical and contemporary urban life is depicted through detailed observations, capturing spatial rhythms and interactions. The artists have delved into East London's evolving culture, reflecting on architecture, societal impact and the emotional aspects of urban renewal and transformation. They have drawn inspiration from local landmarks, including churches, towers and rivers, connecting past and present narratives. The techniques they have used range from archival research and meticulous observation to symbolic and emotional interpretations, highlighting the significance of place and personal experience. Each artist has contributed a unique perspective, resonating with the East London Group's ethos of capturing everyday beauty and the enduring spirit of East End London.

The Urban Contemporaries Group began as an idea by Ferha Farooqui and Frank Creber in 2019, when we brought together figurative painters interested in exploring the urban experience. We have been curating ambitious responses to the subject, responding with drawing as a starting point, painting as the common medium and individual encounters with urbanized life as the dominant motif.

We hope audiences will be captivated by the works on display and the clear link each artist has drawn between their own works and the landscape and passion for this part of London that consumed the East London Group.

Ferha Farooqui & Frank Creber, 2024

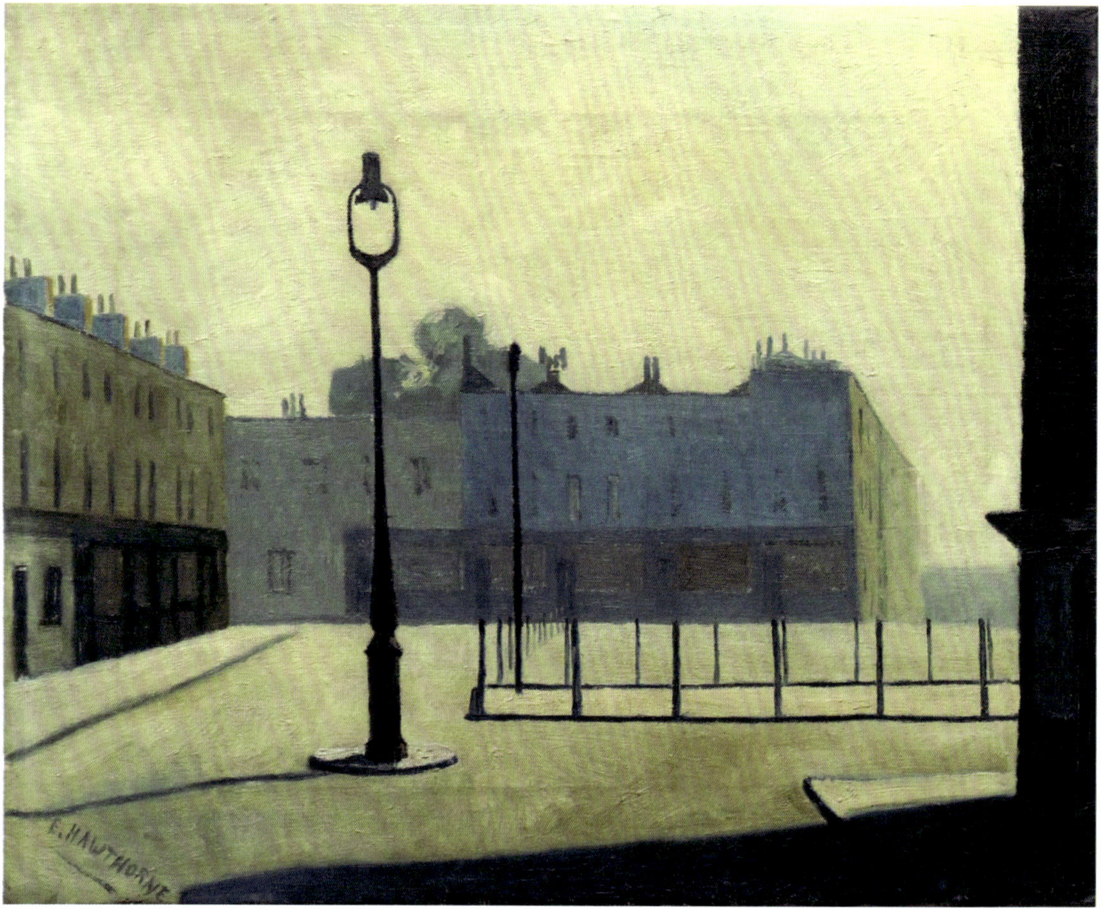

Cumberland Market, Elwin Hawthorne (1931)

This painting was completed during Elwin's third and final year as Walter Sickert's studio assistant. It is, arguably, the most iconic image from the Group's total output. It was once owned by Sir Montague Shearman and, later, by Sir David Scott.

Introduction

by Alan Waltham, curator of the East London Group

This exhibition is the third showing of East London Group work at the Nunnery Gallery. The first one came about as a direct result of the publication of David Buckman's book *From Bow to Biennale: Artists of the East London Group* in 2012.

Through the Group's website, I received a message on Christmas Eve 2012 from Rosamond Murdoch, the Director of the Nunnery Gallery. She said that her partner had bought her a copy of the book and that she'd like to discuss the possibility of putting on an exhibition of the Group's work. Over the Christmas holiday and into the early New Year, we exchanged several emails, and a meeting was set up for 25 January 2013 with David Buckman, Clive Boutle (from Francis Boutle Publishers) and myself to meet Rosamond in the Bow Arts Trust offices at 183 Bow Road. Towards the end of the meeting, Rosamond asked if we'd like to see the gallery space, explaining that it might be a bit of a mess because the space was undergoing major refurbishment.

As it transpired, it really was more of a building site than an art gallery – and freezing cold, to boot! The dates for the show were pencilled in for early March to mid-June 2014. On subsequent visits it became apparent that all the investment and building work had been more than worthwhile, because it had delivered a superb exhibition space.

After the exhibition opened in March 2014, there were numerous events either in the gallery or by way of guided walks in the local area to view some of the painting locations that the group members had used. At one of these events, Frank Creber introduced himself to me. He explained that he was a local artist and tutor working with the Bromley by Bow Centre, and we discussed the possibilities of some sort of collaborative exhibition.

Shortly after the exhibition closed, I began conversations with the gallery team at the Beecroft Gallery in Southend about an exhibition that opened in March 2016. I became distracted by all the arrangements. In the intervening time, I happened to change my email address, and Frank and I lost touch with one another as a result. But in early August 2022 I had a message from Frank, via the Group's website, asking me if I remembered him and if I might be interested in a collaborative exhibition with members of the Urban Contemporaries Group and possibly some guest artists.

We arranged a Zoom meeting, where Frank was joined by Ferha Farooqui, who had been instrumental with him in the formation of the Urban Contemporaries as an exhibiting group. Ferha is also an East London artist, well known for her 'portraits' of lost places and human stories observed on the streets of Newham, in East London, and her work is in public collections including the Guildhall Art Gallery collection and the V&A Print Collection.

As we discussed various ideas with regards to how the exhibition might work, I suggested that the location of the exhibition space would be key. With that in mind, I speculated that the Nunnery Gallery would be ideal because it was centrally located within the East London Group's core area of activity in their formative years and we had exhibited there successfully twice in the past. Therefore, I thought that a fresh proposal might be well received.

Thankfully, my instincts proved to be sound: the Gallery Director, Sophie Hill, was very receptive to the idea, and we quickly moved on to a group Zoom meeting where the basic structure and logistics of the proposed exhibition were agreed, and the project developed from there.

The East London Group artists

During their eight-year career at the Alex Reid & Lefevre Galleries in St James's, London, the East London Group was made up of thirty-three exhibiting members. The majority of them were working men and women from the East End, but their numbers were supplemented by several Slade-trained artists.

During this time, the members showed roughly 730 paintings, with an unspecified number being shown 'ex catalogue'. 46% of those paintings were either landscapes or seascapes, with barely 26% being urban views of the East End or other urban locations further afield. Of that 26%, a significant number are currently 'unknown'; as a result, the pool of work from which this exhibition could be drawn is, unfortunately, limited, but I hope that the work on display gives the viewer a good representation of the various artists' respective talents, styles and abilities. Also, with the 'urban' theme and the relatively restricted area from which the work might have been derived, it has been impossible to include some of the artists whose work was featured in previous exhibitions.

A classic example of this is work by John Cooper, the leader and tutor of the Group, who rarely depicted urban scenes. Of those that he did paint, unfortunately none fall within the scope of this show. At the other end of the scale, Elwin Hawthorne, who was the most productive of the Group members (showing 120 oil paintings in eight years in Group shows, plus 43 in two one-man exhibitions at Lefevre), is the most heavily represented here – partly because his subject matter was predominantly street scenes and urban views, but also because a good proportion of his output has survived into the modern era.

It is worth noting that the seven most productive members of the Group produced between them 520 of the roughly 730 paintings that were exhibited; this fact also presupposes the pool from which work for this show could be drawn. Of the thirty-three members who showed with the Group, twenty produced fewer than ten paintings each, and ten of those produced fewer than two paintings each. It is also interesting to note that, at present, only about 145 of the Group's listed

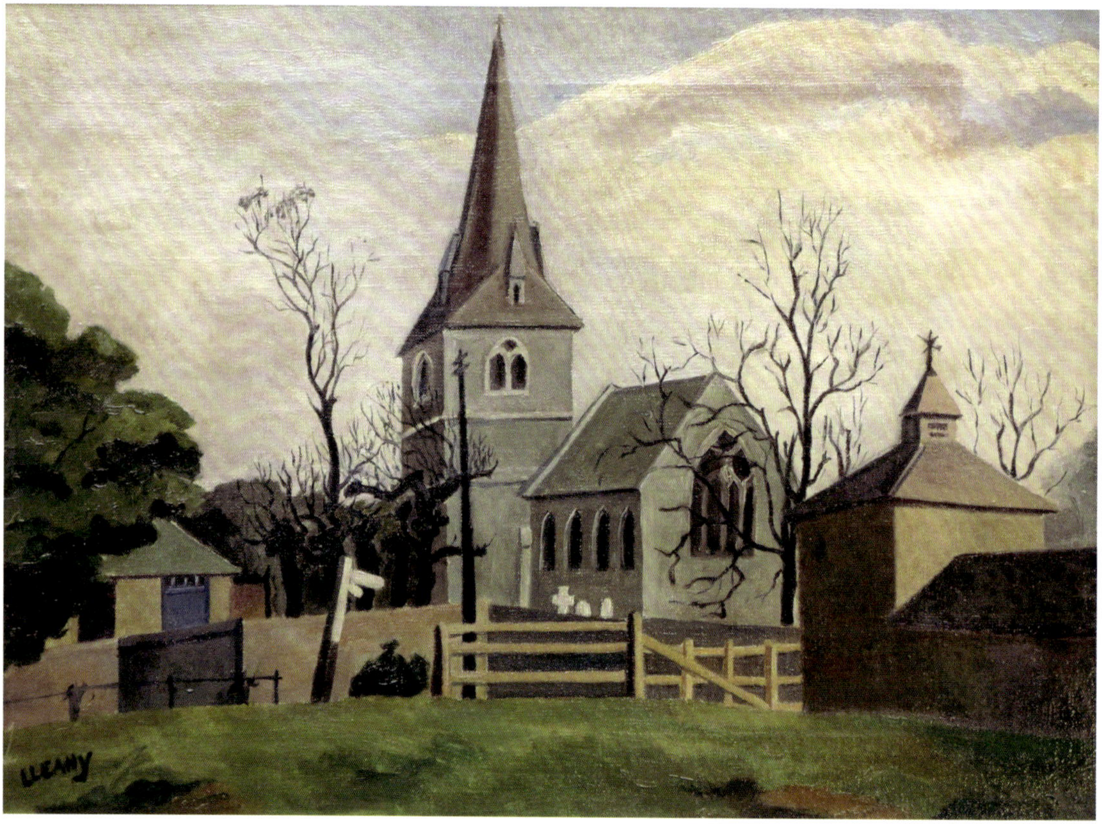

Church at Cranham, Lilian Leahy (1934)

Lilian was a regular contributor to ELG exhibitions but only submitted one or two paintings to each of their eight shows, so surviving examples of her work from the period are rare. Interestingly, both she and her husband-to-be, Elwin Hawthorne, produced views of All Saints Church in Cranham. Quite how they ended up there is a bit of a mystery, because the church is in quite a secluded location – it is possible that they had some sort of particular interest that drew them to the building.

output of paintings are currently known to exist, so potentially there are plenty still out there to be rediscovered. In recent years, since the publication of David Buckman's book about the Group, several pieces of previously unknown ELG work have come to light, and I'm very pleased to say that at least four paintings in this show have not been seen in public in the modern era.

Elwin Hawthorne was a casual labourer and errand boy whose artistic talent was recognized by Walter Sickert when he tutored the East London Group at John Cooper's behest. Sickert employed Elwin as his studio assistant from 1928 until the middle of 1931. No doubt this experience was transformative for the young artist, especially because he was introduced to the art of photography during this period, as Sickert was using it in his artistic practice at that time. The great man's advice to the Group was to 'paint quickly and often'. It appears Hawthorne took this to heart, as is evident from his output. Landscapes and seascapes would feature in Hawthorne's work as time went on, but nearly 70% of his output for Group exhibitions would be street scenes. In common with many other of the Group artists, his work is notable for its general lack of human interest, although some figures do appear.

Walter Steggles left school at fourteen, as was common at the time, and almost immediately started working for the shipping company Furness Withy, where he started as an office boy and then moved into the drawing office. When the family lived in Bath, his parents paid for Wally to have some private art tuition while he was still at school. From a very early age, he had displayed a great interest in art, which he would go on to develop at evening art classes at Bethnal Green Men's Institute, which he joined in May 1925. Later he transferred to the Bromley and Bow Evening Institute when John Cooper moved the classes there in 1926/27. Wally's early catalogue listings show numerous urban subjects and street scenes, but his focus seems to have moved quite quickly towards depicting landscapes and coastal scenes.

Like his older brother Walter, **Harold Steggles** left school at fourteen. He immediately started work as an office boy for a firm of solicitors at Gray's Inn Square in February 1925. In May of that year, he joined the evening art classes at Bethnal Green Men's Institute. He also transferred his allegiance to the Bromley and Bow Evening Institute. Harold kept a diary for a brief period from January to June in 1925, which detailed his transition from school to work. In it he describes his experiences under the tutelage of Mr O'Connor at the art classes. At one point in June, he describes the marking of his work and the comments made by the tutor, which he clearly didn't agree with, stating that 'he is wrong': aged just fourteen, Harold clearly knew his own mind! The exhibition catalogues also show his tendency towards painting landscapes but, unlike his elder brother, Harold's interest in architectural detail meant that his urban work is much more precise in that regard.

The Railway Fence, **Walter Steggles (1929)**
Dating from the first Group exhibition at Alex Reid & Lefevre Galleries, this painting depicts the view of the Great Eastern Railway line at the rear of the Steggles family home at 94 Heath Road at Chadwell Heath. The footbridge is still there but the original Whalebone Lane Bridge has been replaced.

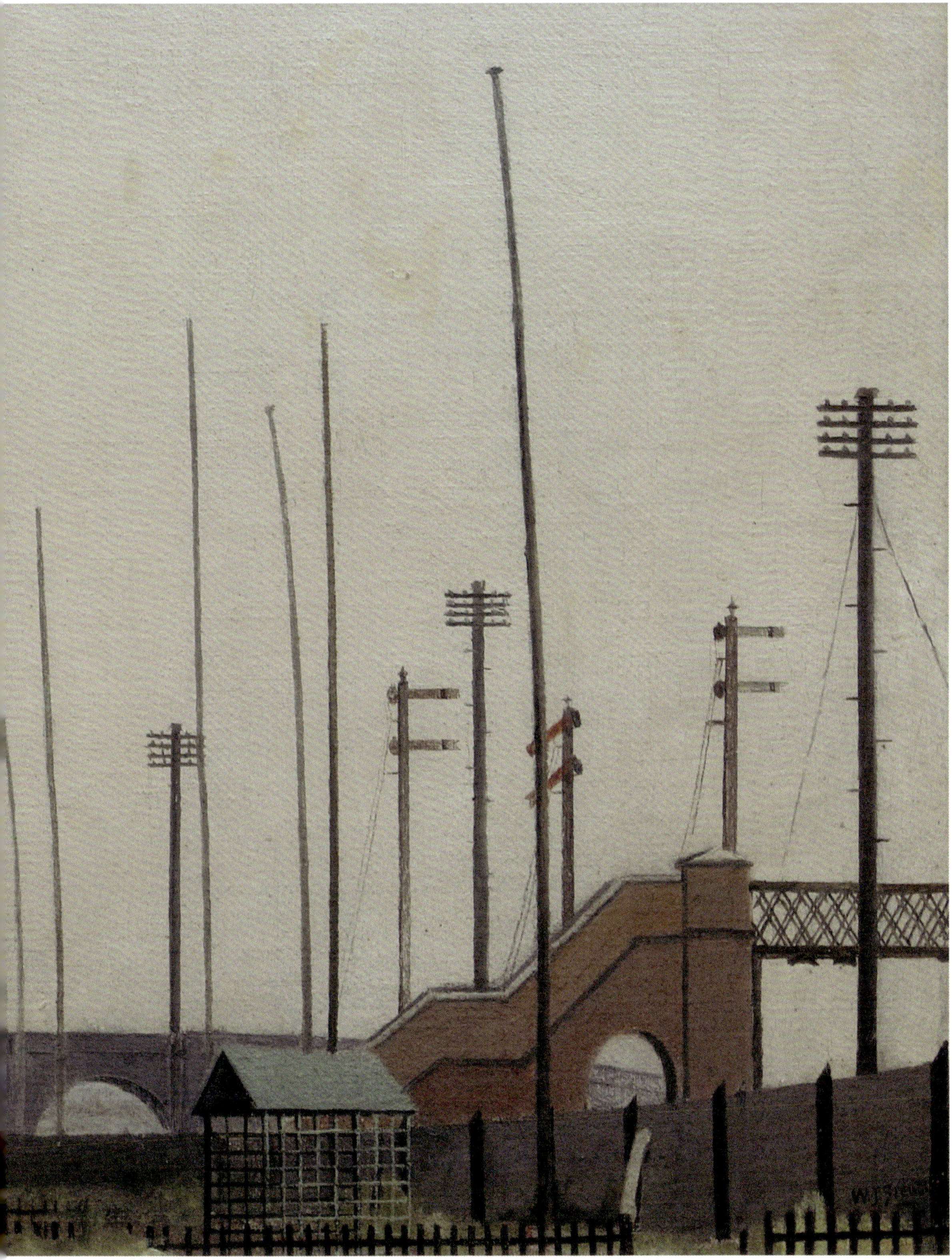

Henry Silk was described by an art critic of his day as one of the most unique artistic talents in Britain at the time. A newspaper interview from 1931 sheds some light on Henry's self-effacing nature as he describes his disbelief, and that of his fellow basket makers, that he was granted a one-man show at the Cork Street gallery of Walter Bull and Sanders Ltd. A large proportion of Henry's surviving paintings are watercolours, a medium in which he excelled and seemingly preferred. He was a bachelor and the uncle of Elwin Hawthorne, from whose mother, Ellen, he rented a room in the Hawthorne family home at 11 Rounton Road in Bow. Having suffered the horrors of service in the trenches on the Western Front during World War I, it seems very likely that Henry suffered with what we would now call PTSD. As a result, he became somewhat reclusive, spending a lot of time in his room, where he took to painting close-up images of many of his personal possessions. Like many of his Group contemporaries, his individual style is instantly recognizable and his work commands a keen following.

One of the female artists of the Group was **Grace Oscroft**, whose father ran an ironmonger's shop at 212 Bow Road. She shared an interest in art with her older brother John, who encouraged her to attend John Cooper's evening art classes at the Bow and Bromley Evening Institute. She showed work at the East London Art Club's exhibition at the Whitechapel Gallery in 1928, at the Tate in 1929, and at each annual Group show at Lefevre from that year until 1936. Judging by the catalogue entries, the majority of her work appears to have been urban views, many of which would have been within walking distance of her Bow home, but towards the end of her exhibiting career occasional landscapes make an appearance. An example of her work is in the collection at The Hepworth Wakefield.

After his service during World War I in both the Army and the Royal Marines, **Albert Turpin** explored various avenues of employment on his return to civilian life. He eventually settled on becoming a window cleaner, partly because the flexibility of the hours allowed him to pursue his hobby of painting, which he had developed during the war. On his way to an evening art class in 1926, he happened to hear a local political activist, Bill Gee, giving a talk; this one event changed the direction of Albert's life. Judging by his catalogue entries, Turpin's work seems to have developed elements of both social and political comment, with titles including *The Prison Gate*, *Sandwich Men* and *Rags*. In 1936, he was deeply involved in the Battle of Cable Street. During World War II, Turpin served in the London Fire Brigade and was made an official war artist. In 1946, he was elected Mayor of Bethnal Green while still working as a window cleaner. True to his values, he eschewed the need to wear any of his official regalia, and while on his window cleaning round he refused the opportunity to clean pub windows because his mother had died of cirrhosis of the liver. Fellow Group member Walter Steggles remembered Albert fondly from when they had sketched together, and commented that 'he was liked by all who knew him'.

Lilian Leahy left school at fourteen. She seems to have had a succession of jobs with an artistic thread running through them, such as window dressing and decorating china and glassware. In her free time she took part in musical productions locally, so her gravitation towards evening art classes was almost inevitable. Like Grace Oscroft, Lilian exhibited at the Whitechapel show in 1928 and then annually with the Group at Lefevre from 1929 until 1936, although she only exhibited nine paintings at the eight Lefevre shows. Lilian married Elwin Hawthorne in 1937. After his untimely death in 1954, aged just forty-nine, she continued to paint in her spare time well into her later life.

The Group membership, comprised mainly of working men and women, was augmented by a number of Slade-trained artists, including **Phyllis Bray**, who had proved to be a star student under Henry Tonks. She exhibited with the Group in their second show at Lefevre in 1930 and would go on to marry the Group's leader and tutor, John Cooper, in 1931. She and Cooper became members of the London Group in 1933. Their daughter Philippa was born a year later but, sadly, the couple separated and divorced only a couple of years later. Through her membership of the London Group, Phyllis met a German refugee, Hans Feibusch. They went on to have a long collaboration, both personally and professionally, as muralists with many prestigious commissions in churches and public buildings across the country. Phyllis exhibited widely in mixed shows and had a highly successful career as an illustrator, working for many publishers as well as companies such as the John Lewis Partnership, London Transport and Shell. Her output in the post-war period was prolific, with many works in both oil and gouache, but her artistic work was cut cruelly short by the onset of Parkinson's disease.

The genesis of the East London Group can be traced back to the first evening art classes at the Bethnal Green Men's Institute in 1924. Among those listed as exhibiting was **George Board**, who would go on to become the only exhibiting member of the Group with work in that first show who would then exhibit with the Group. Little is known about Board beyond the fact that he served in the army throughout World War I, after which he returned to his pre-war employment with Waterlow & Sons Ltd who, among other things, printed banknotes. George was a regular contributor to the Bethnal Green shows as well as exhibiting at the Whitechapel in 1928, the Tate in the spring of 1929, and with the Group at Lefevre in 1929 and 1930. Very sadly, Board's artistic career was cut short when he was made redundant from Waterlow & Sons. With two children, and another one on the way, George was forced to give up painting because he could no longer justify the cost of materials – a sad loss to the art world.

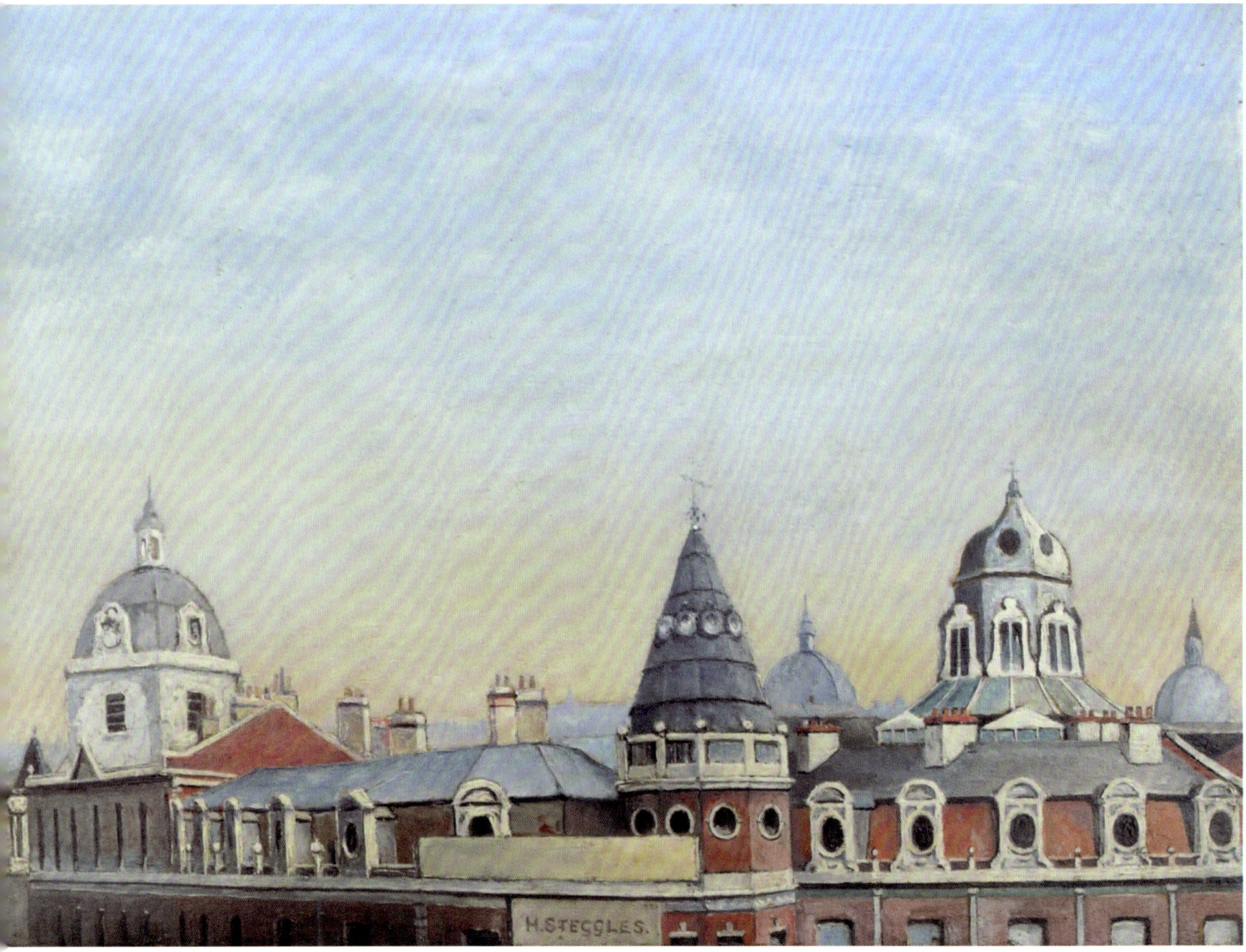

Smithfield Spires, Harold Steggles (1931)

Harold Steggles' regular route to his place of work at Gray's Inn Square, from either Liverpool Street or Fenchurch Street stations, would take him across Holborn Viaduct: this was where this view was taken from.

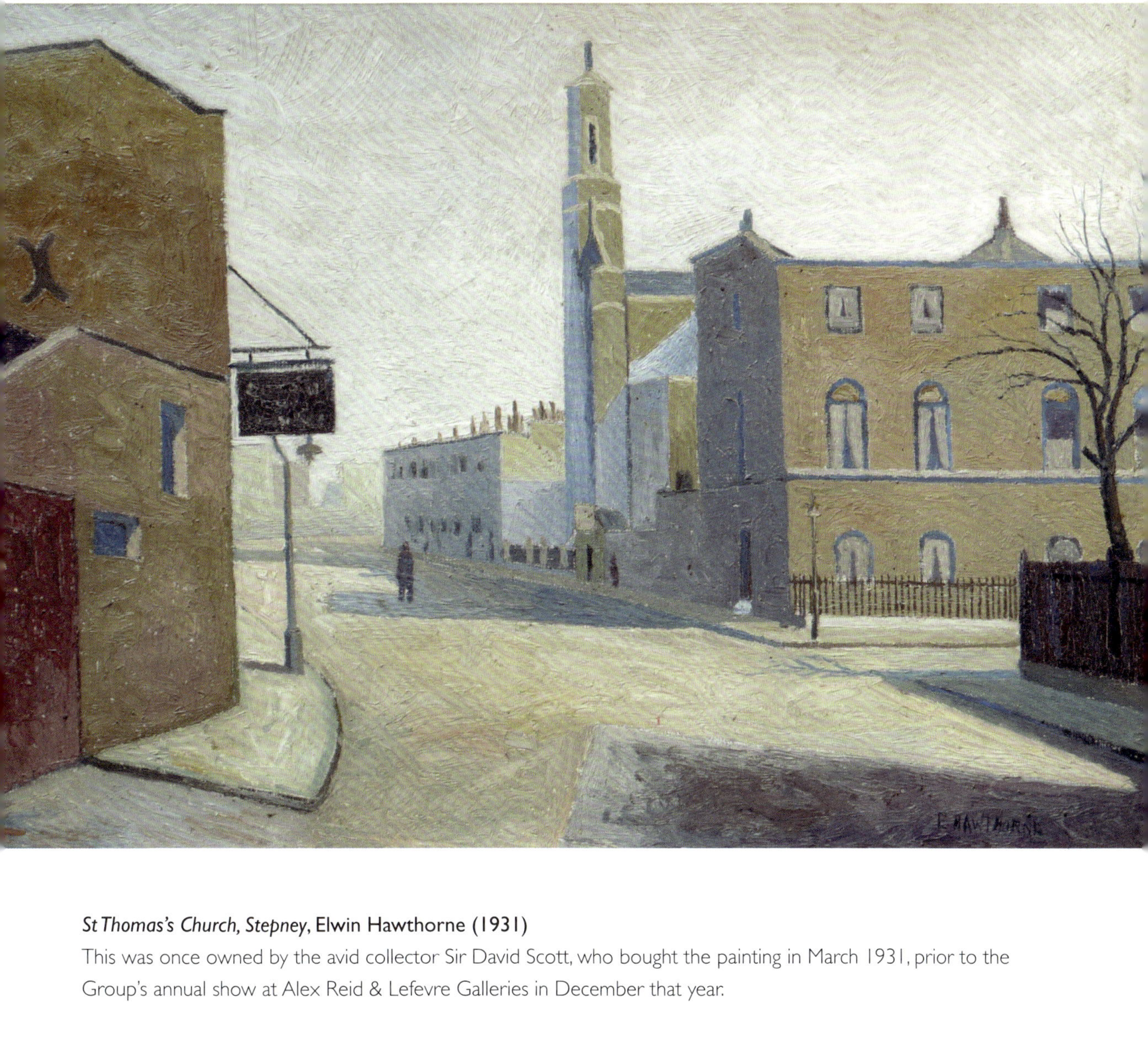

St Thomas's Church, Stepney, Elwin Hawthorne (1931)

This was once owned by the avid collector Sir David Scott, who bought the painting in March 1931, prior to the Group's annual show at Alex Reid & Lefevre Galleries in December that year.

01

North Face I

Artist: David Hepher
Medium: Acrylic, spray paint, concrete on canvas
Dimensions: 227 × 227cm
Date: 2023/24

À la recherche des peintres perdus! Or, remembrance of painters past.

I was unaware of the existence of the East London Group until I was invited to take part in an exhibition commemorating the collective. To me, it had the romantic connotations of the early amateur artists, often Jewish émigrés, who arrived in London at the beginning of the twentieth century, among them Jacob Epstein, Mark Gertler and David Bomberg. Whether they ever showed with the Group is unclear, but they would certainly have been aware of its existence.

Imagine my surprise when the painter Ferha Farooqui kindly sent me images by members of the Group, of whom I had never heard, but who had painted the local landscape in and around East London. They were marvellous, understated visual documents of the city and how it looked. Why is it that we never hear of such artists today? There was Utrillo in Paris, and Hopper in New York, but here the establishment, terrified of being thought provincial, looked the other way. During my lifetime, Lowry has grudgingly been acknowledged, as was, briefly, Algernon Newton by a show at the Royal Academy in the early 1980s. Apart from that, the powers that be prefer to ignore what is on their doorstep. Yes, we have Sickert, but he is remembered more as a painter of general subjects than of the cityscape.

To me, someone who shares the love of the Group's local cityscape, this opportunity was a gift. I've always painted the environment I find myself in – whether in France, where I paint the fields, or London, where I paint the buildings! What has changed since those early days is the vertical scale of the architecture and the very evident sense of 'life' as shown by the ever-changing graffiti and general urban mess. A kind of abstract expressionism seems to descend upon the face of the city, celebratory and alive, but the 'doing' of which is never seen.

I try to make work that reflects this exuberance and combine it with its physical materiality, at the same time telling the story of how it looks. The other difference with the early works is the absence of cars: the streets look curiously empty; tidy, even. There is a gentle, discreet suggestion of geometric abstraction in *Bow Road* by Elwin Hawthorne (1932) and in his *The Guardian Angels* (1931). Of course, this is echoed in the paintings of Nash and Ravilious – who were painting at the same time – which shows that they were fully aware of the wider context of their work.

To answer my own question as to why so many of these very genuine amateur artists are forgotten, I suppose the reply would be that they add nothing to the development of the language of painting. In a mild, Fauvist way, the Camden Town Group did, as did the Euston Road Group in terms of a kind of measured figuration, but always ever so well mannered. Other than that, there have been individuals – such as early Auerbach, Kossoff, and Adrian Berg's *Regent's Park* paintings – but no groups!

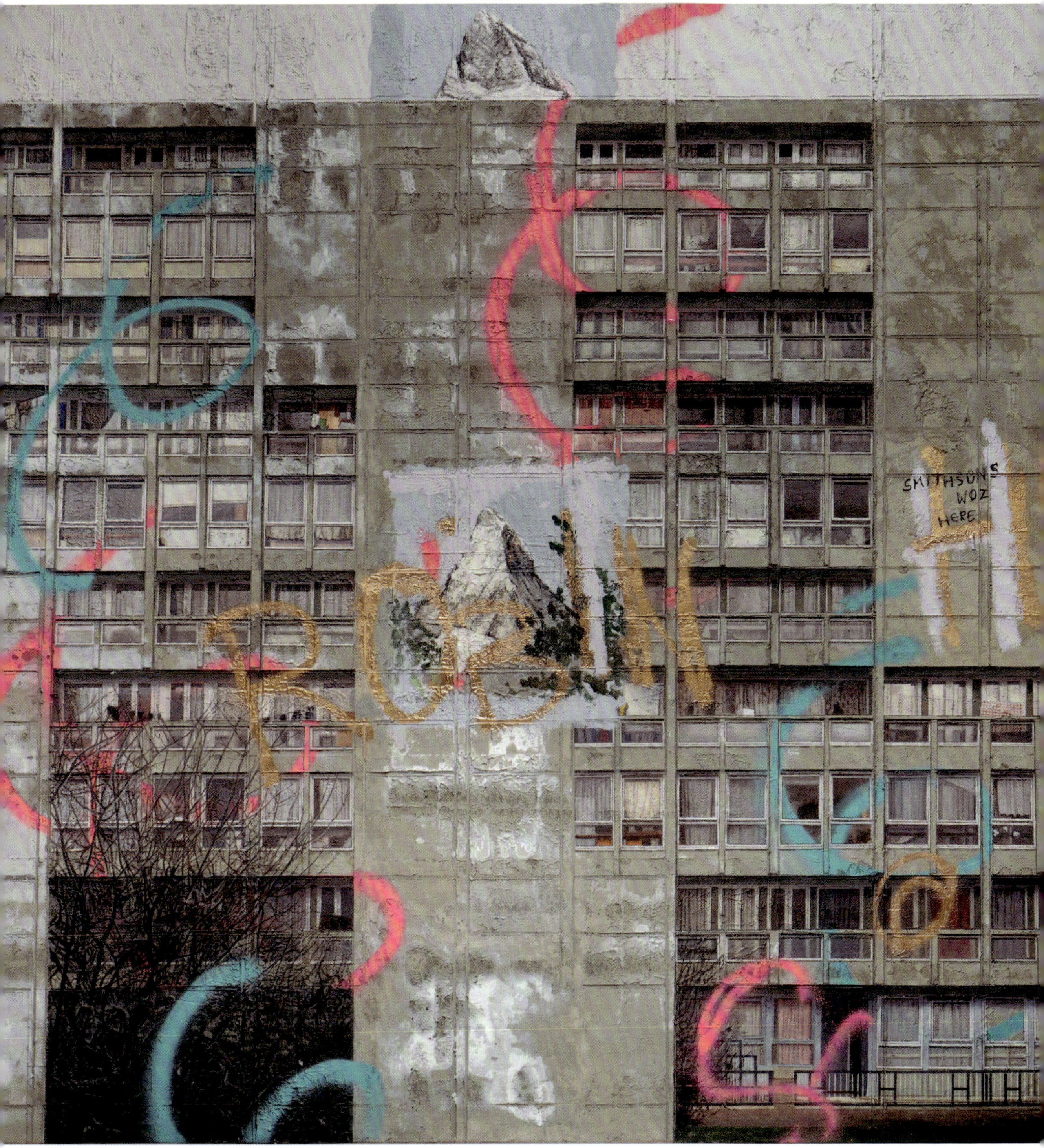
SMITHSONS
WOZ
HERE

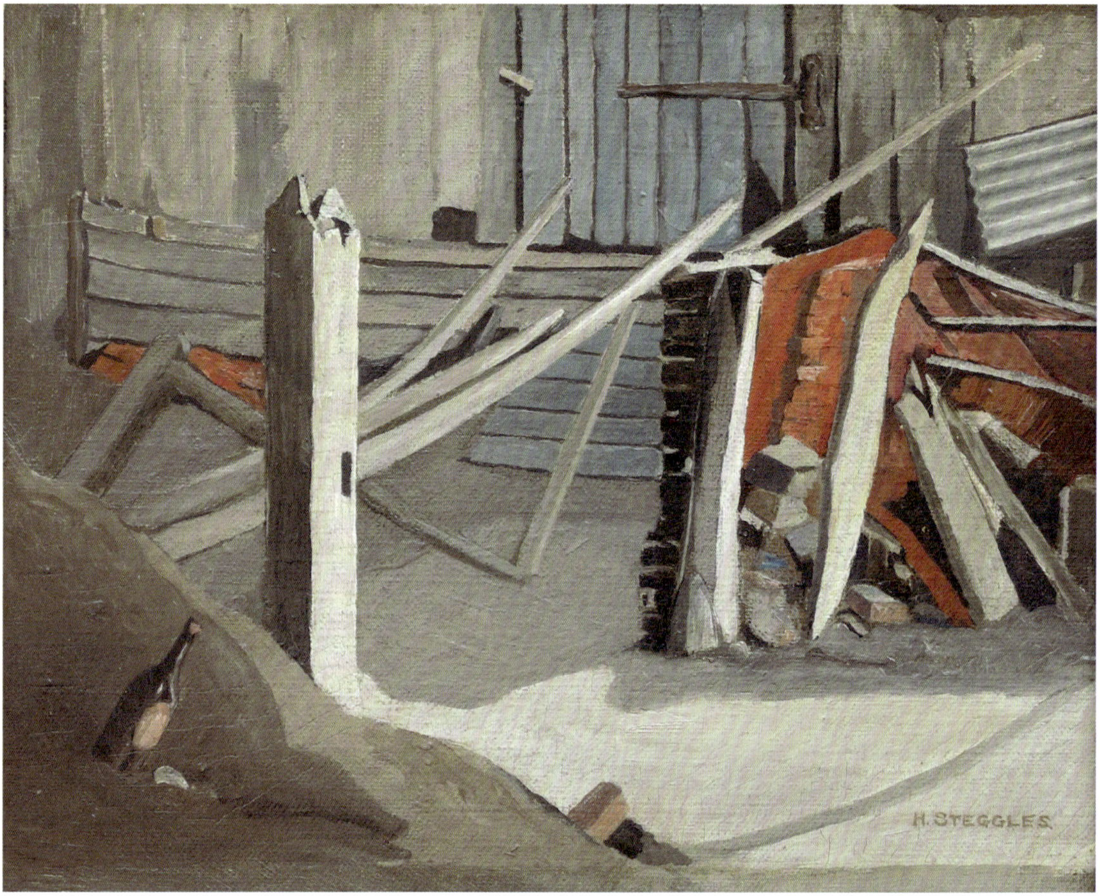

The Lumber Yard, Harold Steggles (1929)

This painting featured in the first Group exhibition at Alex Reid & Lefevre Galleries. The curving lengths of timber in the painting look remarkably like the shafts from an old farm cart, so this scene may have been painted at Lamb's Farm, not far from 94 Heath Road, Chadwell Heath, where the Steggles family were living at the time.

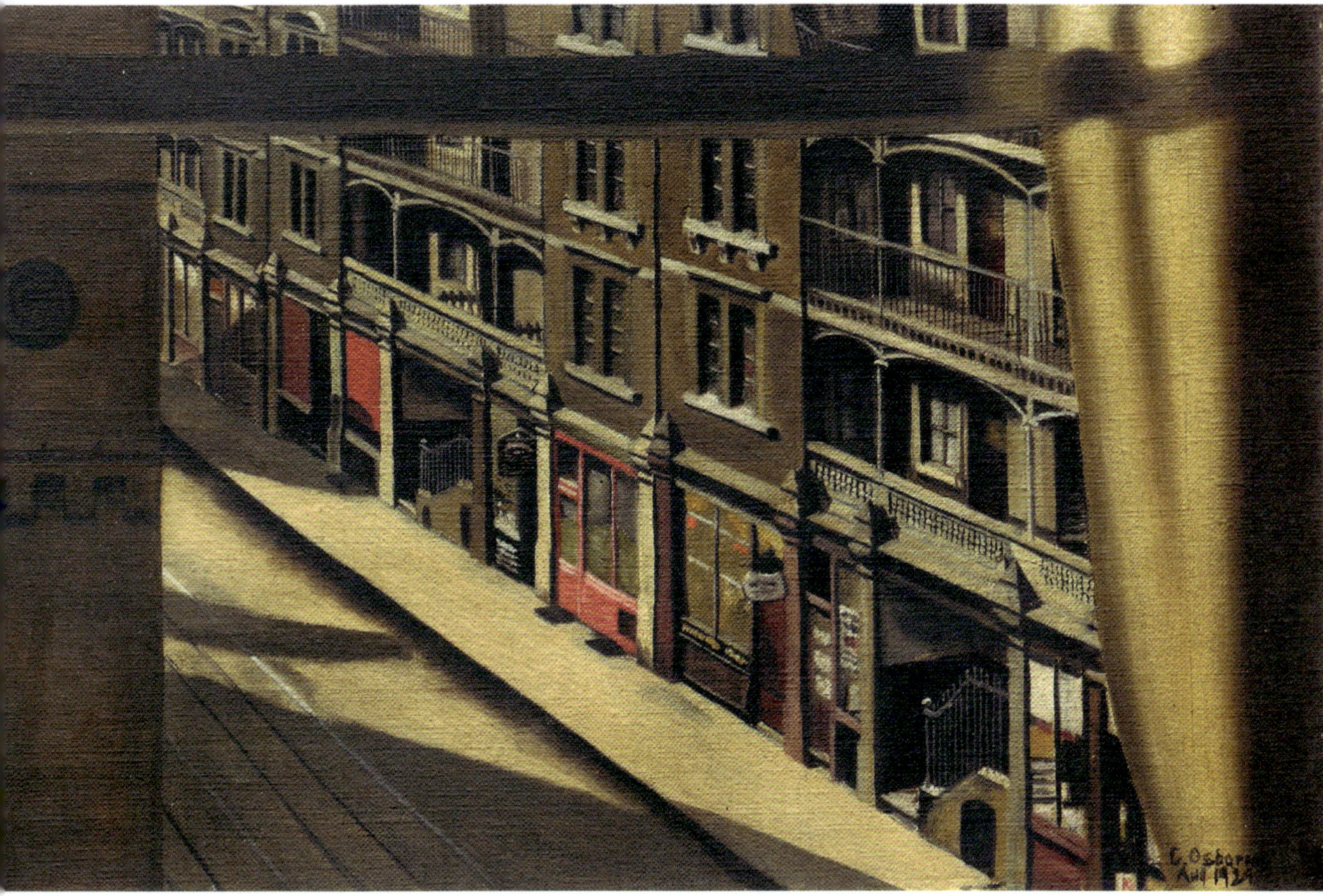

Sunday Morning, Farringdon Road, Cecil Osborne (1929)

This is an iconic East London Group image but, for a long time, the location depicted was uncertain. Thankfully, a positive identification was made a few years ago – the painting shows the Corporation Buildings (demolished c.1970) at 119–141 Farringdon Road. Cecil was living on the opposite side of the road at 221 Farringdon Road Buildings, so this would have been the view from his window.

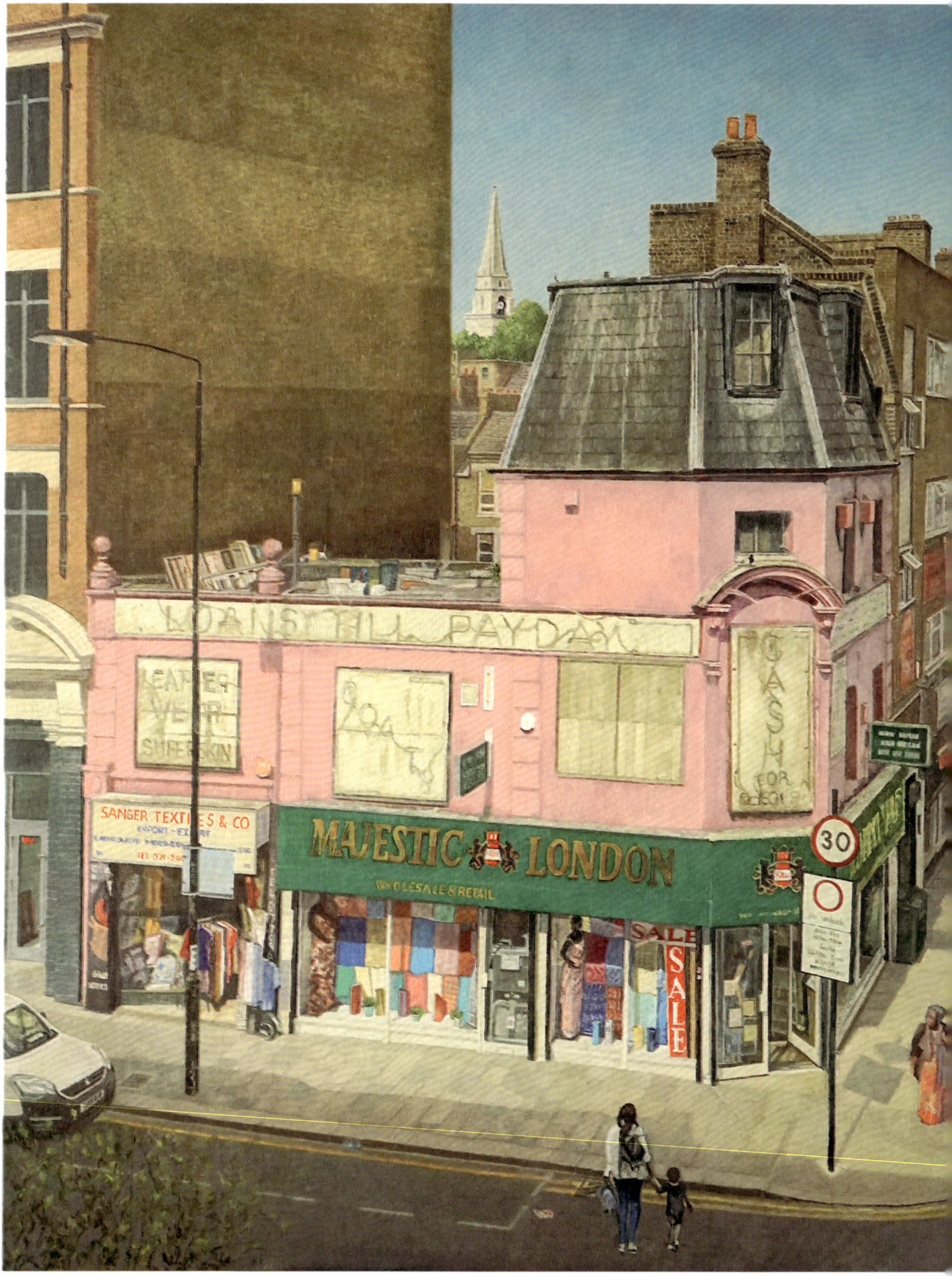
MAJESTIC LONDON
WHOLESALE & RETAIL
SALE
SALE
30

02

Lost in Spitalfields

Artist: Doreen Fletcher

Medium: Oil on canvas

Dimensions: 100 × 80cm

Date: 2024

When I moved to the East End in 1983, I had no idea of the existence of the East London Group, nor that I was following in the footsteps of other artists who, a generation earlier, were interested in the same content as myself. Had I been aware of their work, I would have been intrigued. Treading a path as an urban landscape painter during the 1980s and 90s was considered to be too representational, although I was accepted into the Whitechapel Open a few times.

I became aware of the East London Group in 2013. A friend recommended a visit to an exhibition of their work entitled 'Now and Then' at TownHouse, Spitalfields. I was taken by both the location and the work. I went on to read David Buckman's book *From Bow to Biennale* with great interest. Since then, I have had five solo shows at TownHouse, exhibiting paintings of my own interpretation of East London. Of course, over time, the meaning of what defines East London has spread as populations have moved along the estuary, thus bringing Dagenham, Basildon and Southend into the scope of its culture.

I am delighted to be invited to participate in 'Following in the Footsteps of the East London Group' at the Nunnery Gallery – even more so as I had an exhibition there myself in 2019: 'Doreen Fletcher – Paintings'.

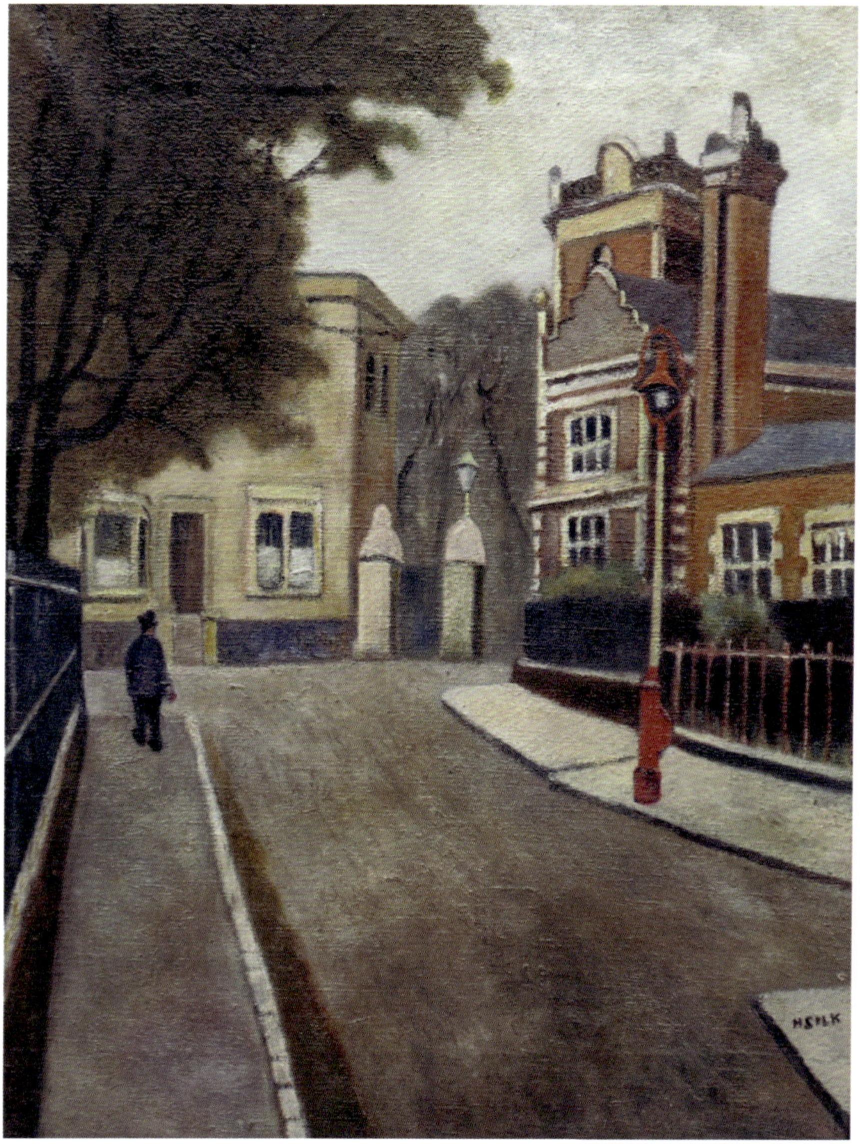

St James's Road, Old Ford, Henry Silk (1933)

Now known as St James's Avenue, this view shows a scene that no longer survives of the very distinctive lodge houses that were at various entrances to Victoria Park, this one being at the Bonner Hall Bridge. Very sadly, the lodge was destroyed by enemy action in 1941 but, thankfully, the wrought iron gates and posts still survive.

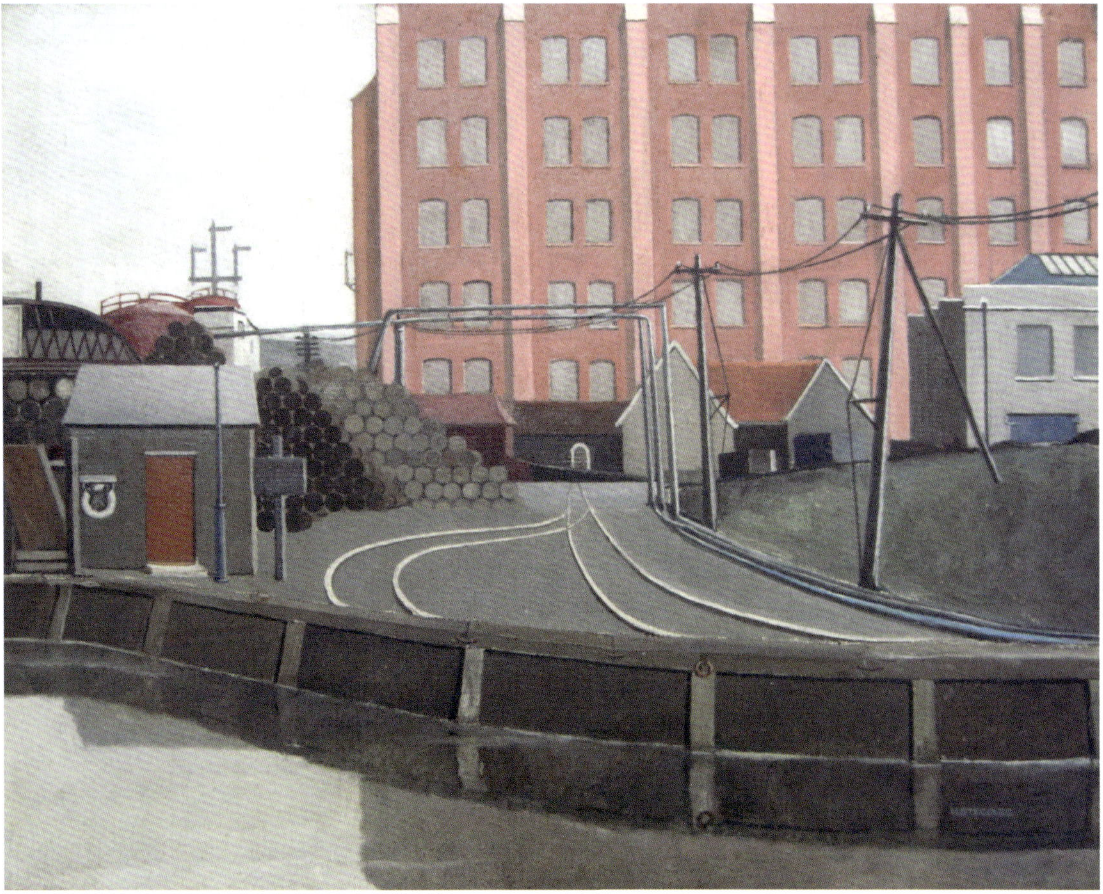

Wharf Houses, Harold Steggles (undated)

According to Harold Steggles' catalogue listings from the period, he never exhibited a painting with this title. He did, however, show *Brewery Yard* in 1930. Interestingly, when it was listed by the Contemporary Art Society in their Annual Report from 1930/31, it was listed as *Quayside Warehouse*, but by W J Steggles rather than Harold! The Accession Records at Brighton, dated October 1933, show that the title was then listed as *Wharf Houses* and, correctly, that it was painted by H Steggles.

03

Moving East

Artist: Ben Johnson

Medium: Acrylic on canvas

Dimensions: 100 x 142cm

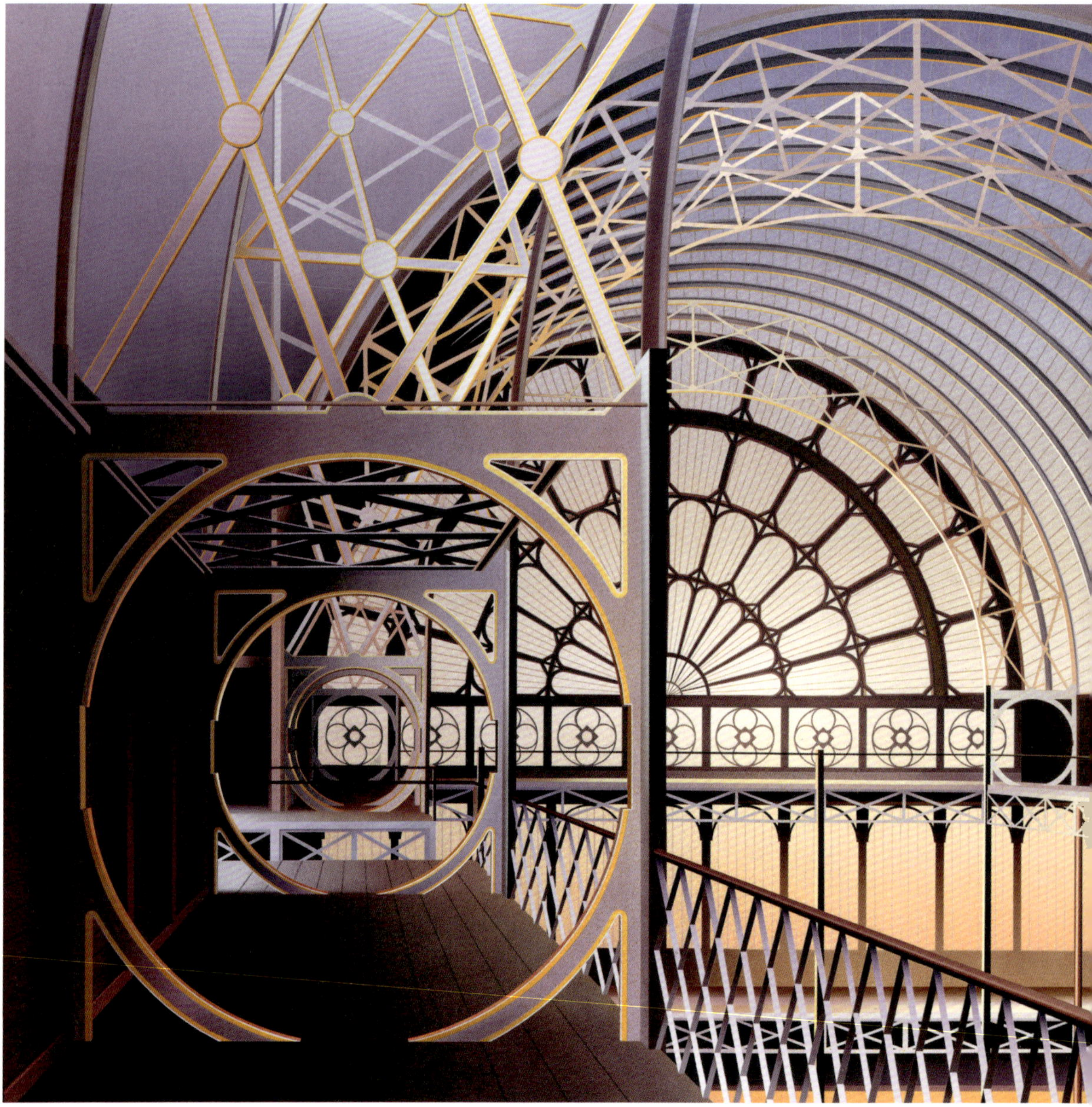

Moving East is a celebration of the invention, ambition and creativity of working-class East London artists and craftspeople of a bygone age, and the importance of art in a civilized society.

In 1851, the Great Exhibition took place in Hyde Park, in the Crystal Palace. This was a major exhibition of art, industry and manufacturing, and probably the most influential cultural event of the nineteenth century. The extraordinary building that was the Crystal Palace was dismantled, and a section of it was moved to South Kensington to become part of the early Victoria and Albert Museum. In 1870, this same section was moved to Bethnal Green to form the East London Museum of Science and Art. Its intention was to diffuse knowledge of science and art in a community that was predominantly made up of mechanics, labourers and tradespeople – people used to surviving by hard work and practical skills. This building is now the Young V&A.

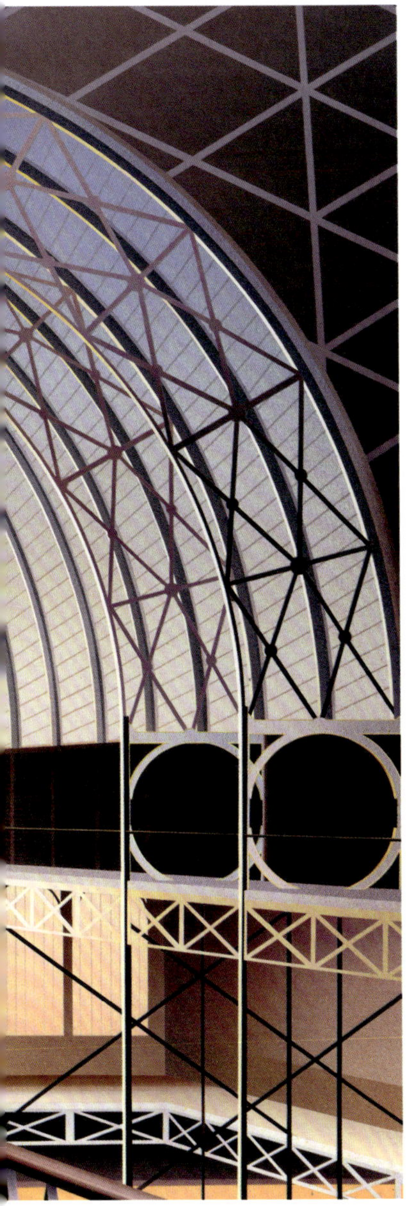

The V&A continues to move eastwards, and this year will open in the Olympic Park, Stratford. My painting's title refers to this journey. Between 1928 and 1936, the mostly working-class realist painters known as the East London Group developed from an art club based in Bethnal Green. They questioned their surroundings and were inspired by its architecture. Many had stopped their education at elementary school level, just like Joseph Paxton, who had left school aged twelve to become a gardener's assistant before becoming the architect of the Crystal Palace, one of the world's most inventive and inspiring structures. It seems totally appropriate that Bethnal Green should have inherited a structure that looked to the future and celebrated the man-made.

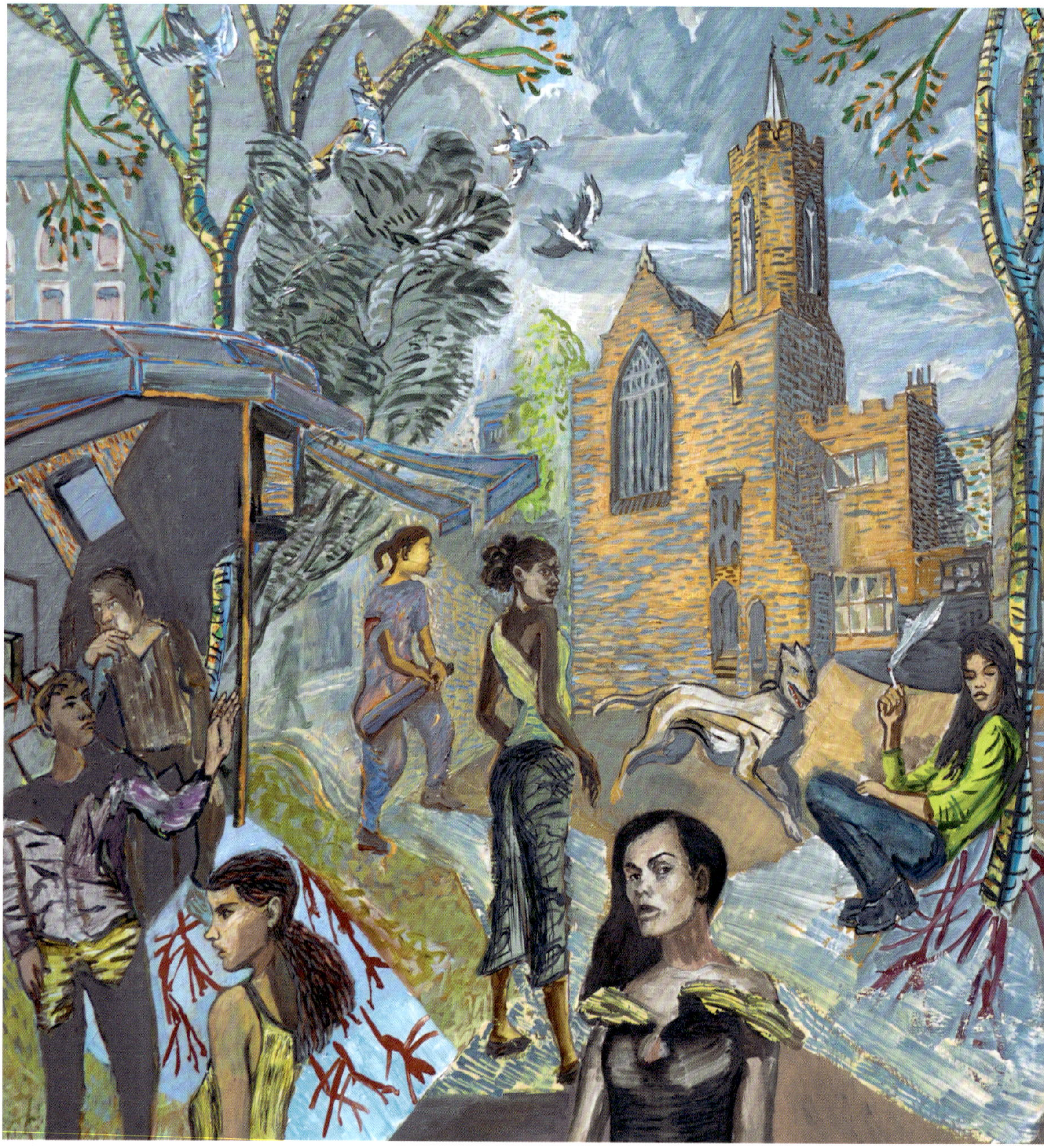

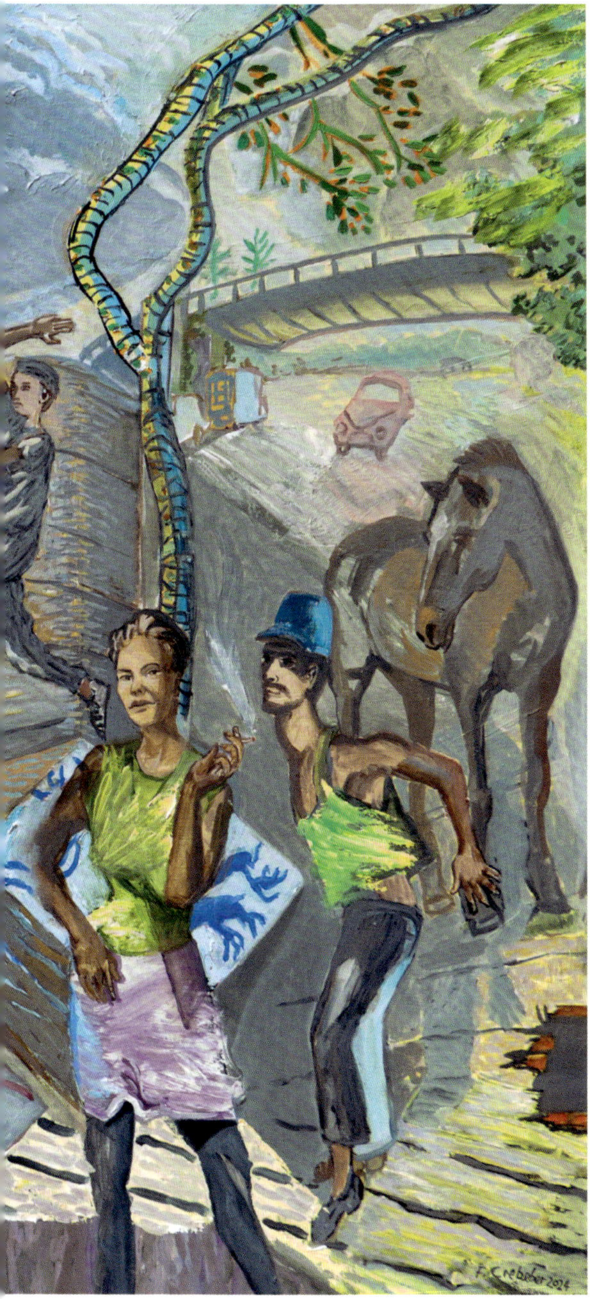

04

The Limping Man Clue

Artist: Frank Creber

Medium: Oil on canvas

Dimensions: 85 x 130cm

Date: 2024

I chose to paint the Guardian Angels Church in Mile End in response to the painting by Elwin Hawthorne. The narrative in my painting comes from a story in the *East London Advertiser*, Saturday 27 May, 1939:

> LIMPING MAN CLUE. Four Years for Mile End Cigarette Theft. A hole big enough for a man to fit through was knocked in the basement wall of a Mile End shop. 280,000 cigarettes, valued at £607, were stolen. A horse and a loaded cart led by a man with a limp were seen from the rear of the shop.

I set out to make a painting about Mile End with the church and the Yellow Bridge. At the same time, I was researching the work of the East London Group and, considering the experience of people living in East London in the 1930s, I wanted to make a connection across the ninety years of time. I began looking at newspaper stories of East London in the 1930s, looking for an eye-catching story that could become a narrative for the painting. The story about the thief who stole cigarettes was unusually visual, and grabbed my imagination.

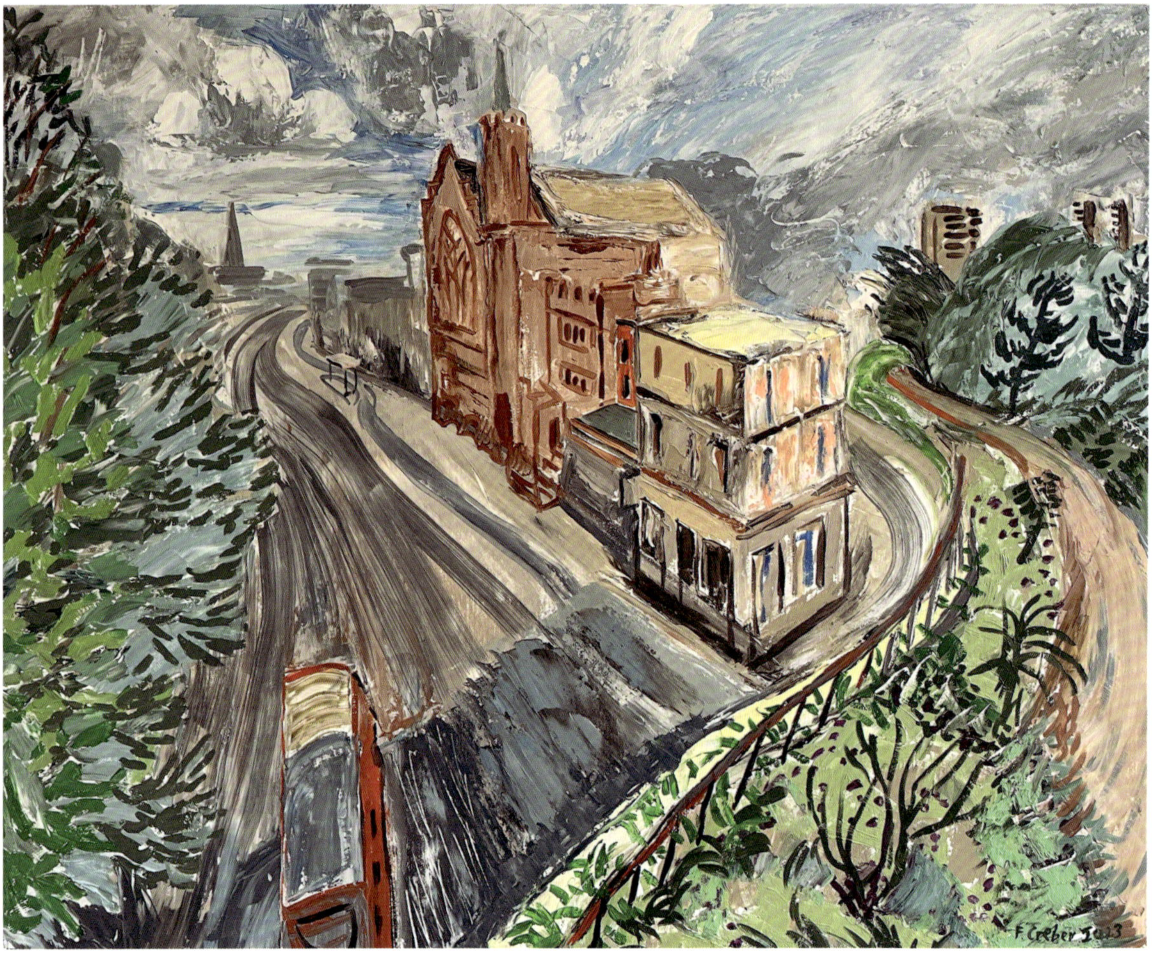

Plein air painting of Guardian Angels Church, Frank Creber (2023)

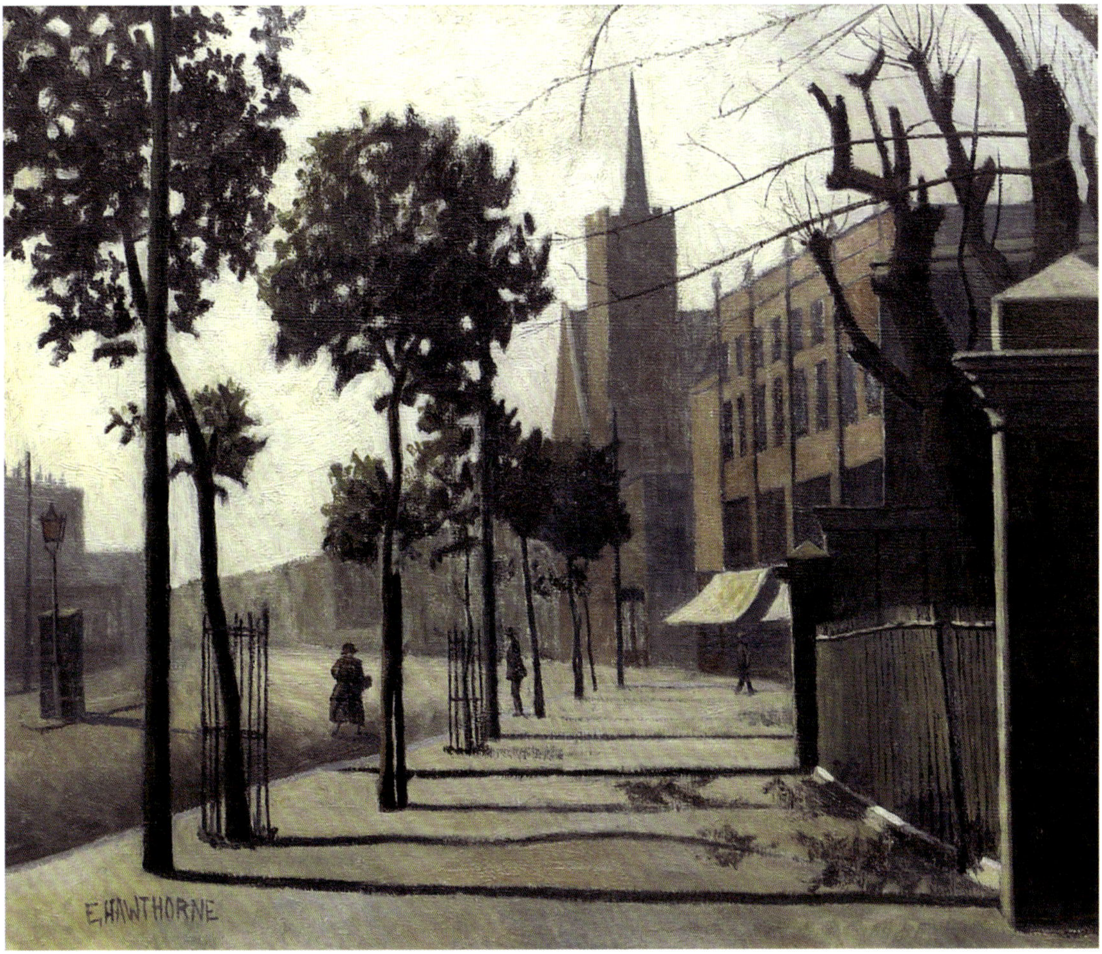

The Guardian Angels, Elwin Hawthorne (1931)

An archive photo of this scene exists, showing this view. Elwin's notes detail that it was painted 'from corner of Cottage Grove'. Sold from exhibition, it resurfaced at auction on the continent some years ago and now resides back in the UK.

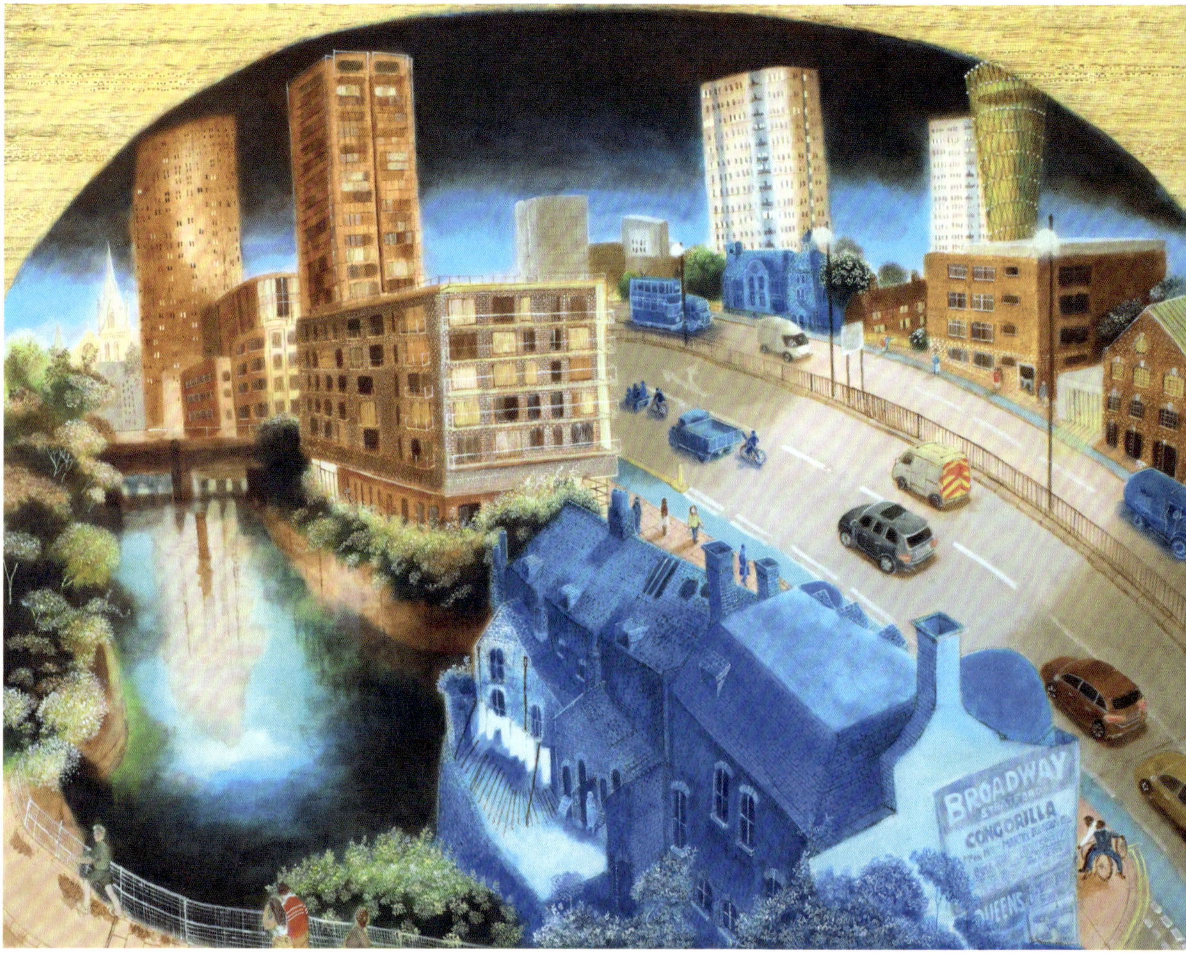

05

Lost Highway

Artist: Ferha Farooqui

Medium: Acrylic glaze on wood panel

Dimensions: 90 × 122cm

Date: 2024

My painting attempts to chronicle the changing environment of East London and the lived realities of the contemporary population. *Lost Highway* is a 'timescape' of Stratford, in Newham. For many years, I have been noticing how time is found in the environment in buildings and fragments of the detritus of earlier generations. This painting depicts the drama of the urban high street. It is a composition based on observations of everyday life and photographic archives, culminating in a 'portrait' of the lost places and human stories observed on the streets of Newham, in East London, where I've lived (almost continuously) since the early 1970s.

In this painting, I've been discovering the signs and remains of edifices, objects and people from the past and have animated the painting with ghostly shadows of these vanished places and people. The luminous blues represent absent things

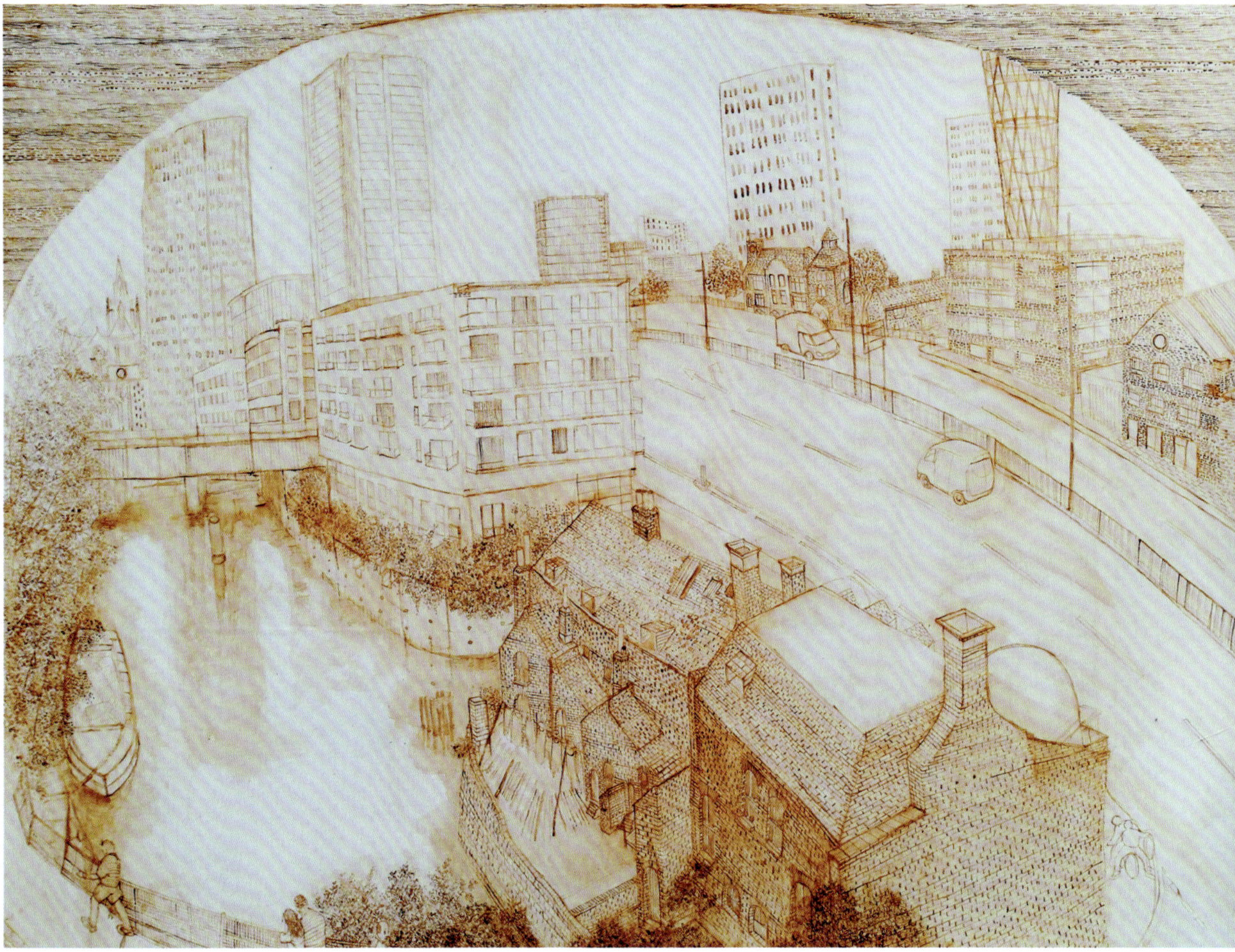

Lost Highway in progress, Ferha Farooqui (2024)

rediscovered in my research and then placed back into the environment. The blue edifices are shadows of missing buildings – the former Harrow public house and cottages on Stratford High Street – while in the distance is the High Street Stratford Board School (destroyed in the Blitz), echoing *Bow Bridge* and *Stratford* by Walter Steggles.

The blue figures are former inhabitants who once walked the same streets, and appear to mingle among the present-day population. Co-curating this exhibition has allowed me to walk in the 'footsteps' of this early generation of working-class London painters and reinstate scenes they might have observed over a hundred years ago, while evoking a perception in the viewer of the continuous transformation of the urban landscape and the correlation between the past and the present.

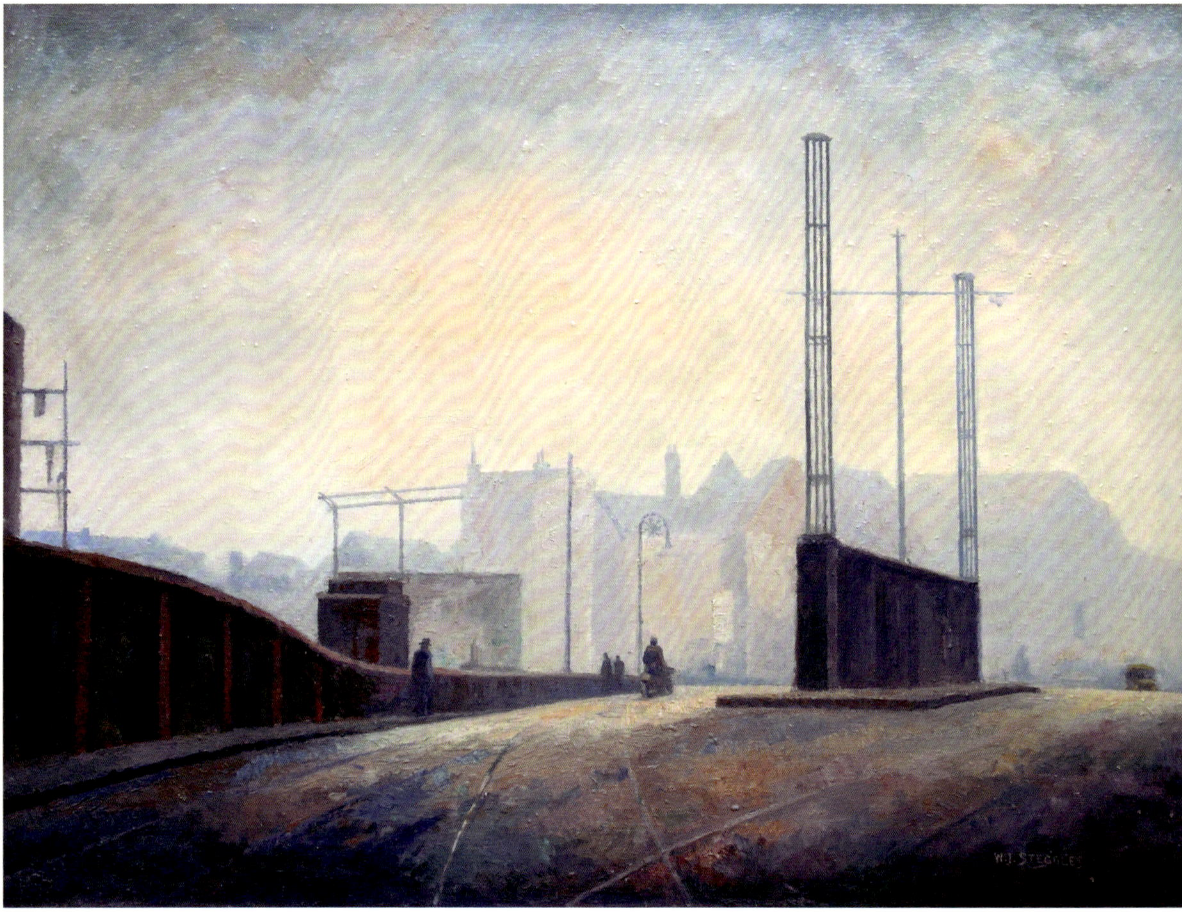

Bow Bridge, Walter Steggles (undated)

Walter Steggles does not appear to have listed a painting with this title in his studio book, but the image very loosely mirrors a known sketch of his that is annotated with the inscription 'Blackwall'. However, several key details are different. It is possible that Walter had sight of an archive photo of the view, courtesy of his best friend Elwin Hawthorne, who painted *Demolition of Bow Brewery* from a similar viewpoint.

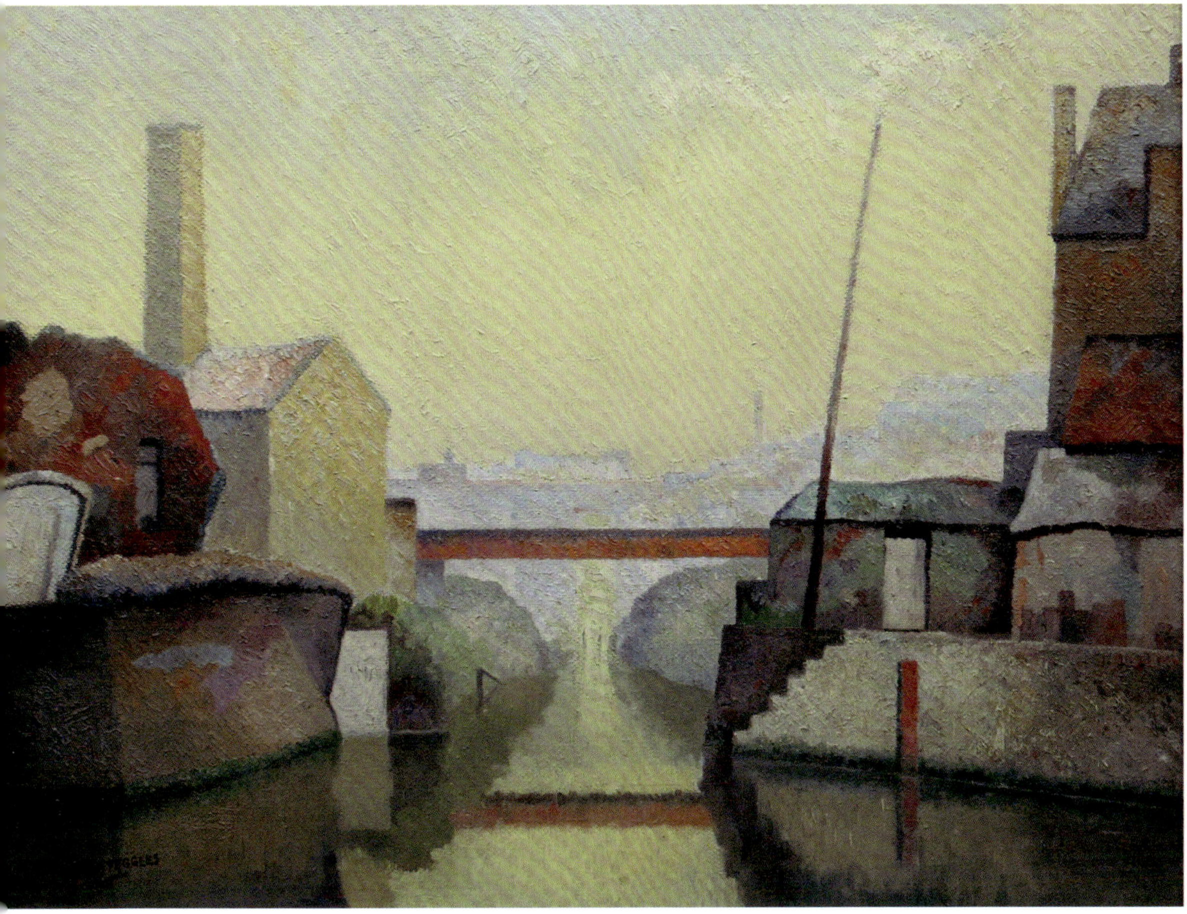

Stratford, Walter Steggles (1938)

A photo of this view exists in Elwin Hawthorne's archives, showing us that Walter Steggles painted what he saw. This painting was shown at Alex Reid & Lefevre Galleries in a joint show between Walter and his younger brother Harold in 1938. Judging by the fact that Walter revisited this image in later life, it was obviously a scene that he enjoyed painting.

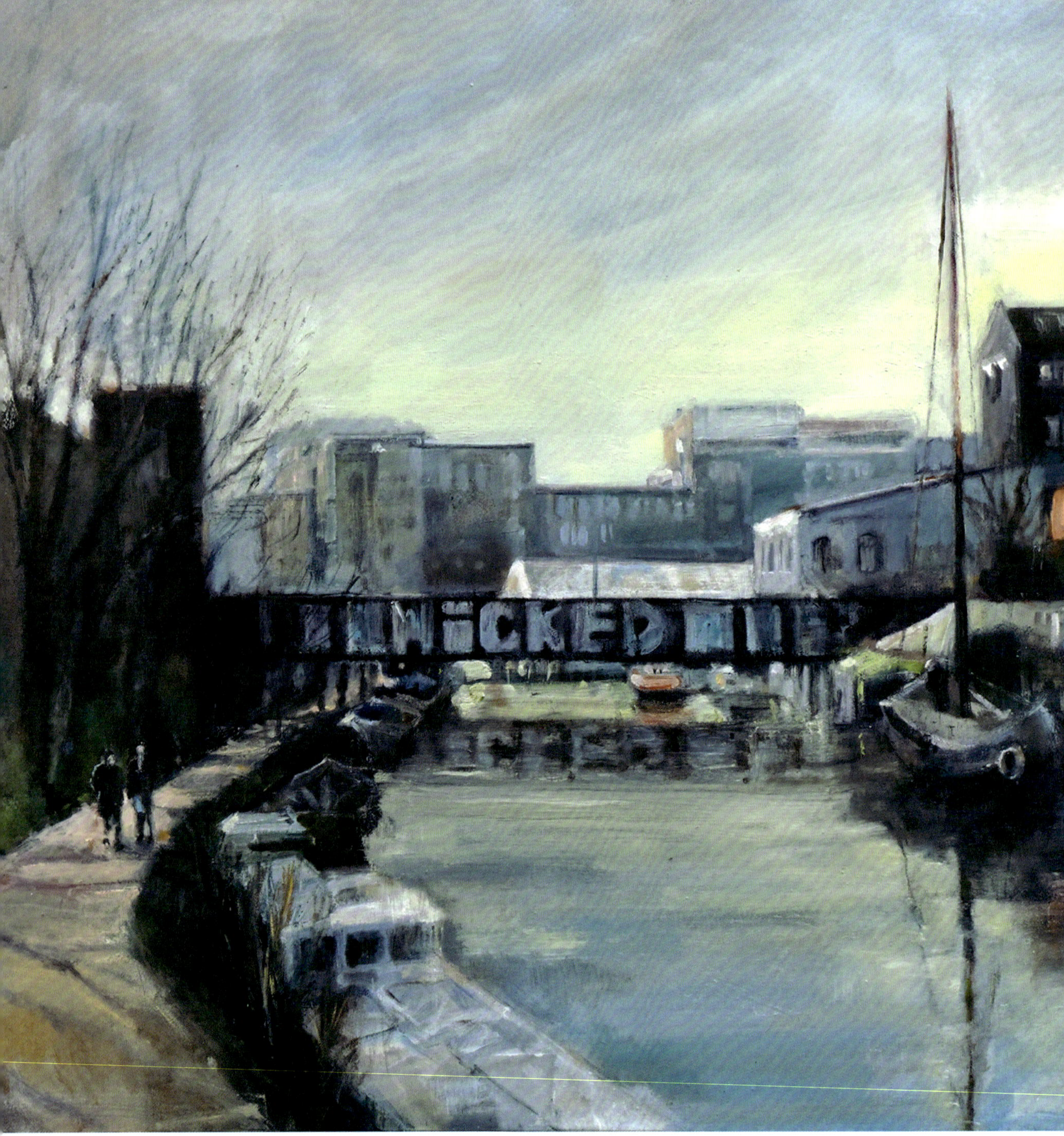
WICKED

06

Wicked

Artist: Sarah Lowe

Medium: Oil on canvas

Dimensions: 60 x 60cm

Date: 2024

I have lived in East London and the suburbs along the River Lea most of my life, and was drawn to Walter Steggles' *Stratford* because of the way he presents the river and contrasts it with the industrial features in the painting. The colour palette also resonates with me. The reflected red bridge and the hard edges of the urban buildings contrast with the soft pale lemon light on the river.

My own work reflects on the transient nature of cities, looking at both the human connection and the beauty of ordinary landscapes impacted by those who inhabit them. The river, however, remains a ubiquitous presence.

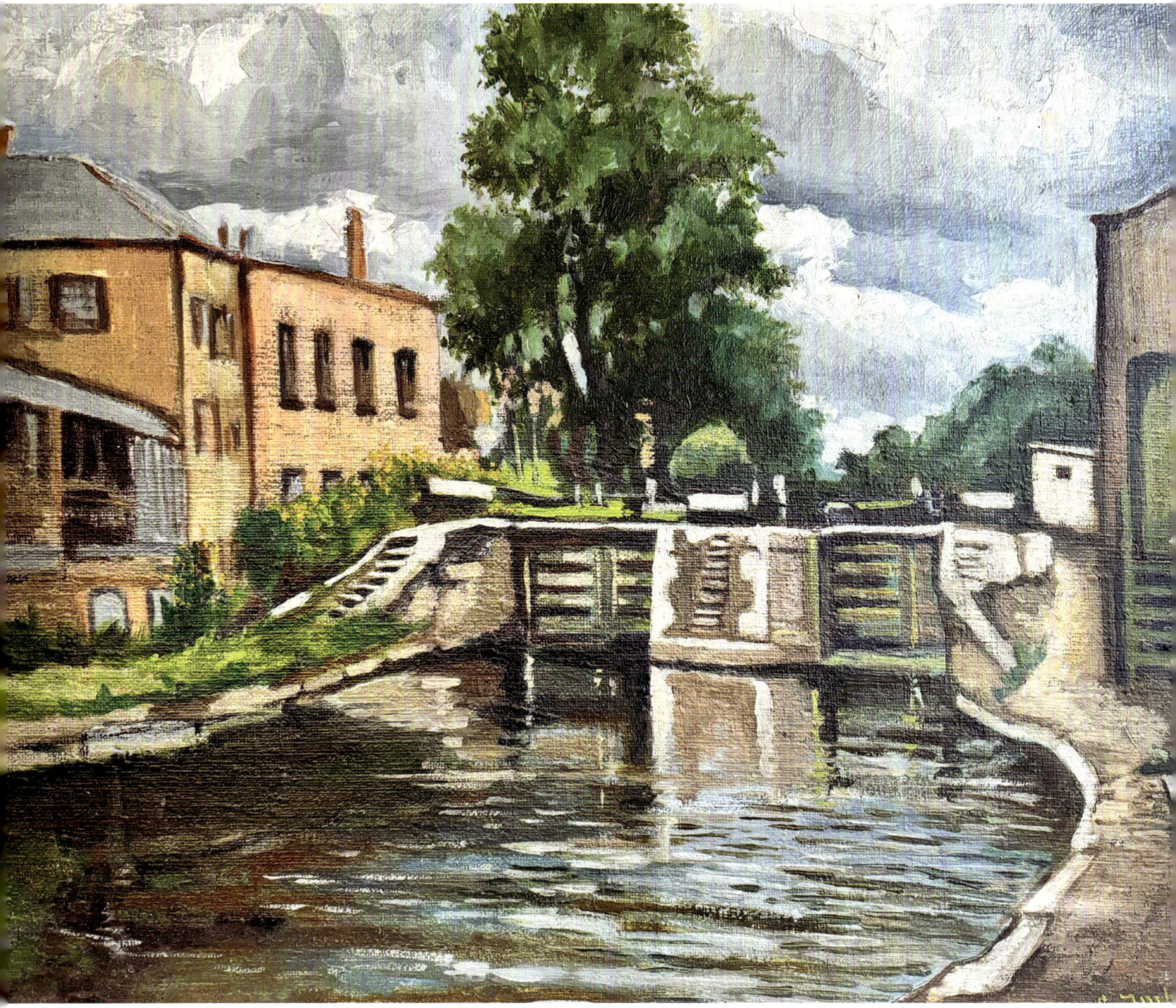

Old Ford Lock, Albert Turpin (undated)

Albert seems to have had quite an affinity with canals as they feature in several of his later works. He would still be able to recognize the majority of this view today, which is good to see. Albert continued to work as a window cleaner after serving as Mayor of Bethnal Green and, according to his daughter Joan, he would often go out on Sunday mornings to sketch and paint.

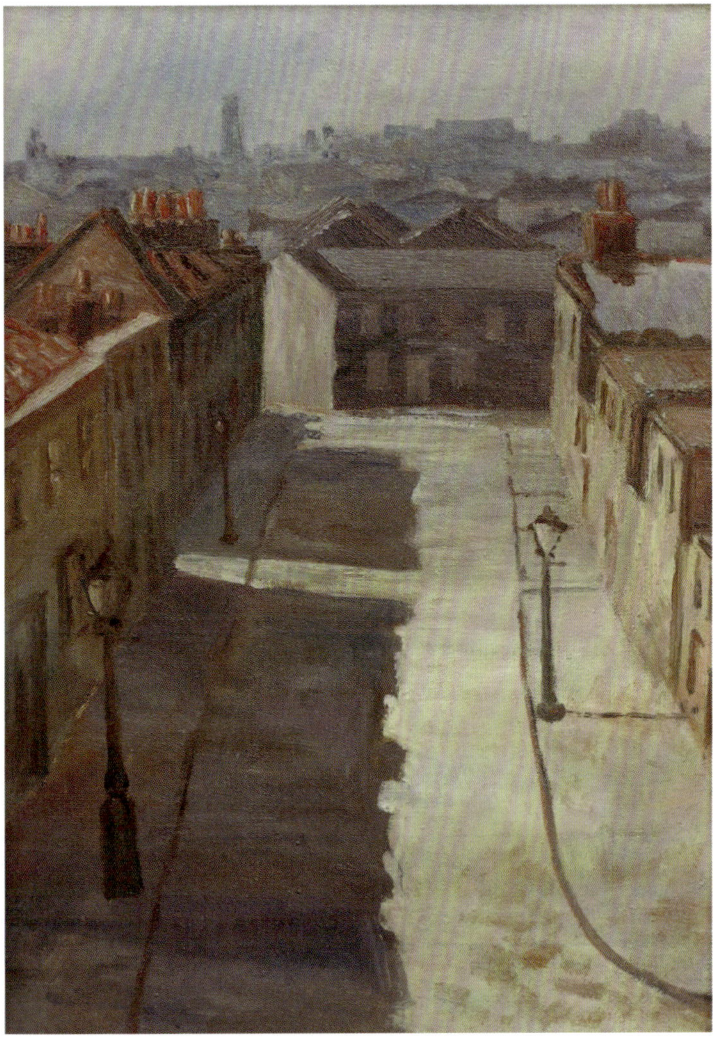

N.E. Bethnal Green, George Board (1928)

The precise location for this painting is, sadly, unknown, although it is possible that this was a view from the school in Wolverley Street where the evening art classes were held. Another alternative is that it might have been a view from the Guinness Trust Buildings on Columbia Road where George lived at around that time. There has been some discussion suggesting that it may have been painted in moonlight, judging by the faint glimmer from the streetlamps.

07

Cambridge Heath Road

Artist: Michael Johnson

Medium: Oil on canvas

Dimensions: 112 x 127cm

Date: 2023

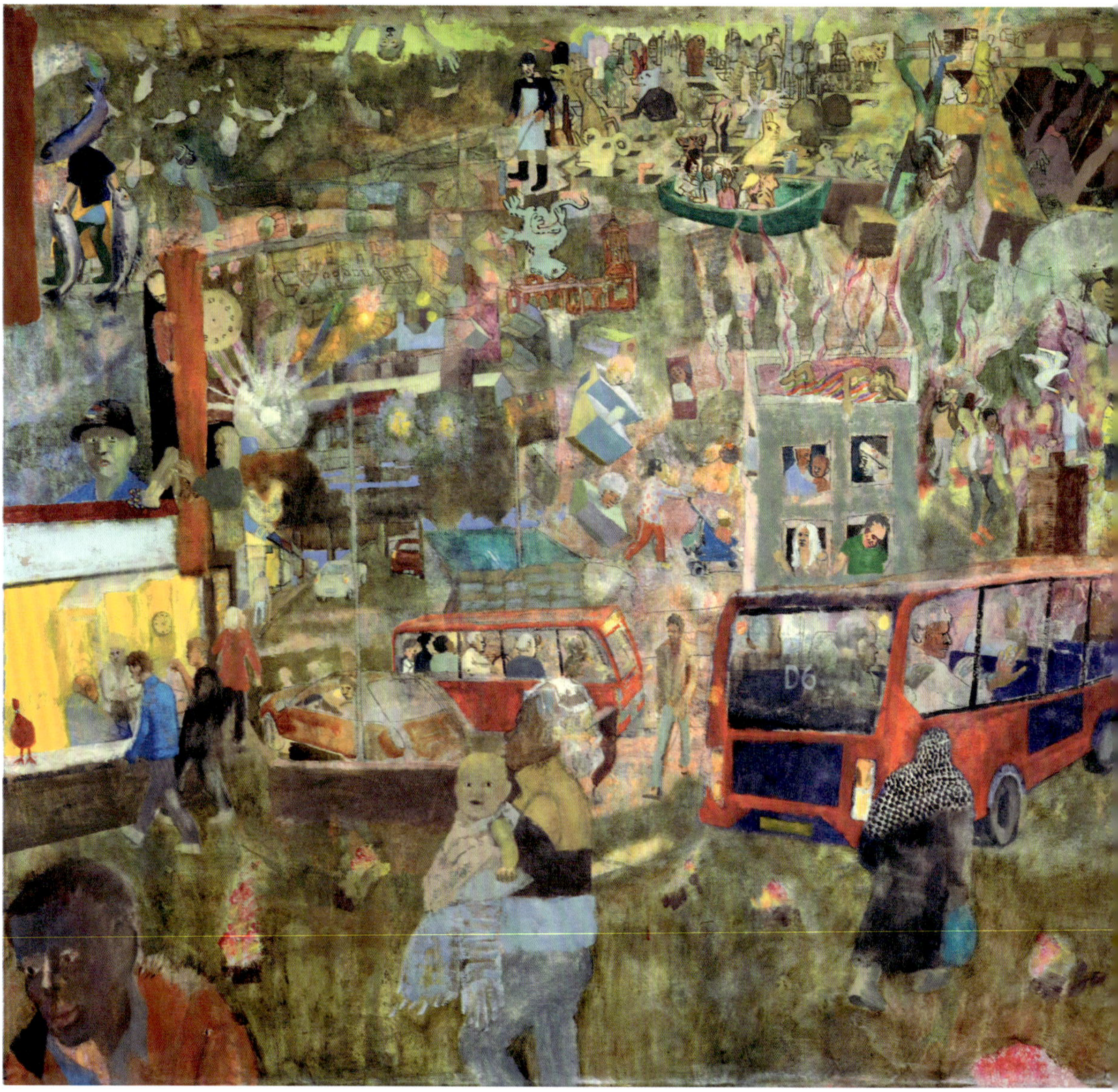

I chose the painting of northeast Bethnal Green by George Board because I like the viewpoint: the intimacy of the street in the foreground combined with a distant skyline. London has always inspired me on the local and panoramic level simultaneously. Also, I know the area well, having lived and worked there.

I sketched at street level, and on buses. The motion of the bus induces a kind of reverie, scenes revealed cinematically as glimpses into the past and present. I quickly sketched fellow passengers, sometimes while talking to them, as with the foreground man and woman. I was very aware of the trainline to Cambridge passing over the junction, a sense of ancient filaments of intellectual, religious and mercantile life. A distant view of the City of London becomes a view of a rewilded Cambridge Heath (agricultural land until the mid-eighteenth century); a graveyard of real and mythical creatures.

East London left an indelible impression on me when I first arrived in the capital in the mid-1980s. I regularly cycled between my flat in West London and my brother's flat on the Isle of Dogs. The East End resonated with the echoes of centuries of sea trade and hard labouring. The docks, undergoing development, reeked evocatively of spices they'd traded. My father would reminisce about his engineering apprenticeship in East London in the 1950s. It is an area I find inspiring for its family, poetic and human associations.

08

Trinity Green Chapel

Artist: Grant Watson

Medium: Oil on aluminium

Dimensions: 65 x 39.3cm

Date: 2024

Many of the scenes the East London Group painted have now vanished; however, I liked the challenge of painting a building that still exists, the main difference being only time.

My first thought was to bring my newly acquired box easel to the Almshouses to paint in the open and respond directly to a subject that had been painted so beautifully by Elwin Hawthorne back in 1935. I wanted to make my own intimate and personal response. It was a slow start and difficult to make a meaningful connection with the building, which, along with the distractions from talkative passers-by, made me think again.

Back in the studio, in between drawing, I began to fold bits of cardboard. Before I knew it, the process of making a model of the Almshouses' chapel had started. Its construction felt very similar to the way I draw and paint: adding a little bit here and taking away there. In making the sculpture, I discovered an intimacy with the building that had been lacking before. With just me and the building in the studio, I could concentrate without distraction. I painted and drew while I sculpted too, each activity in dialogue with one another. Sculpting felt like drawing, and painting felt like building. With the model, I was not restricted by viewpoints; I could look from above, below, or from any given angle. The forms and shapes became increasingly familiar, and emotional connections were discovered.

The sculpture stands as an artwork in its own right but also as a catalyst for making the painting on show. The painting is a combination of encounters with both the physical building, with all the hustle and bustle surrounding it, and the model, which sits serenely in the studio ready for contemplation.

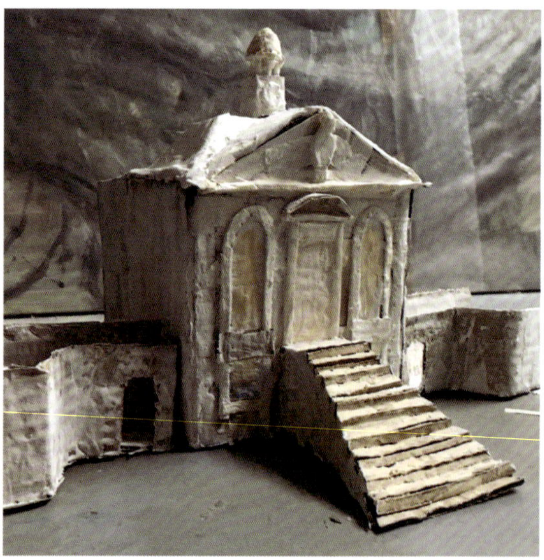

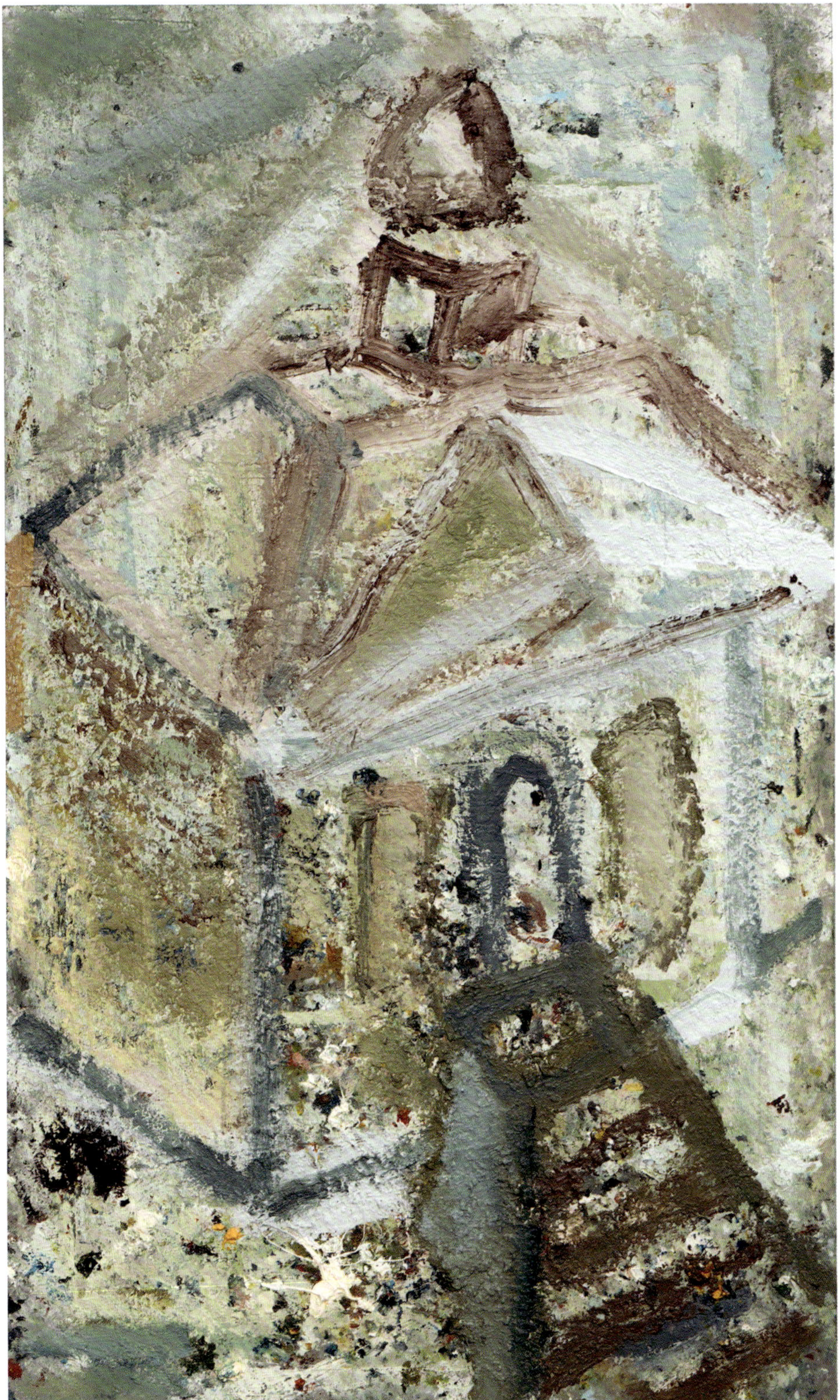

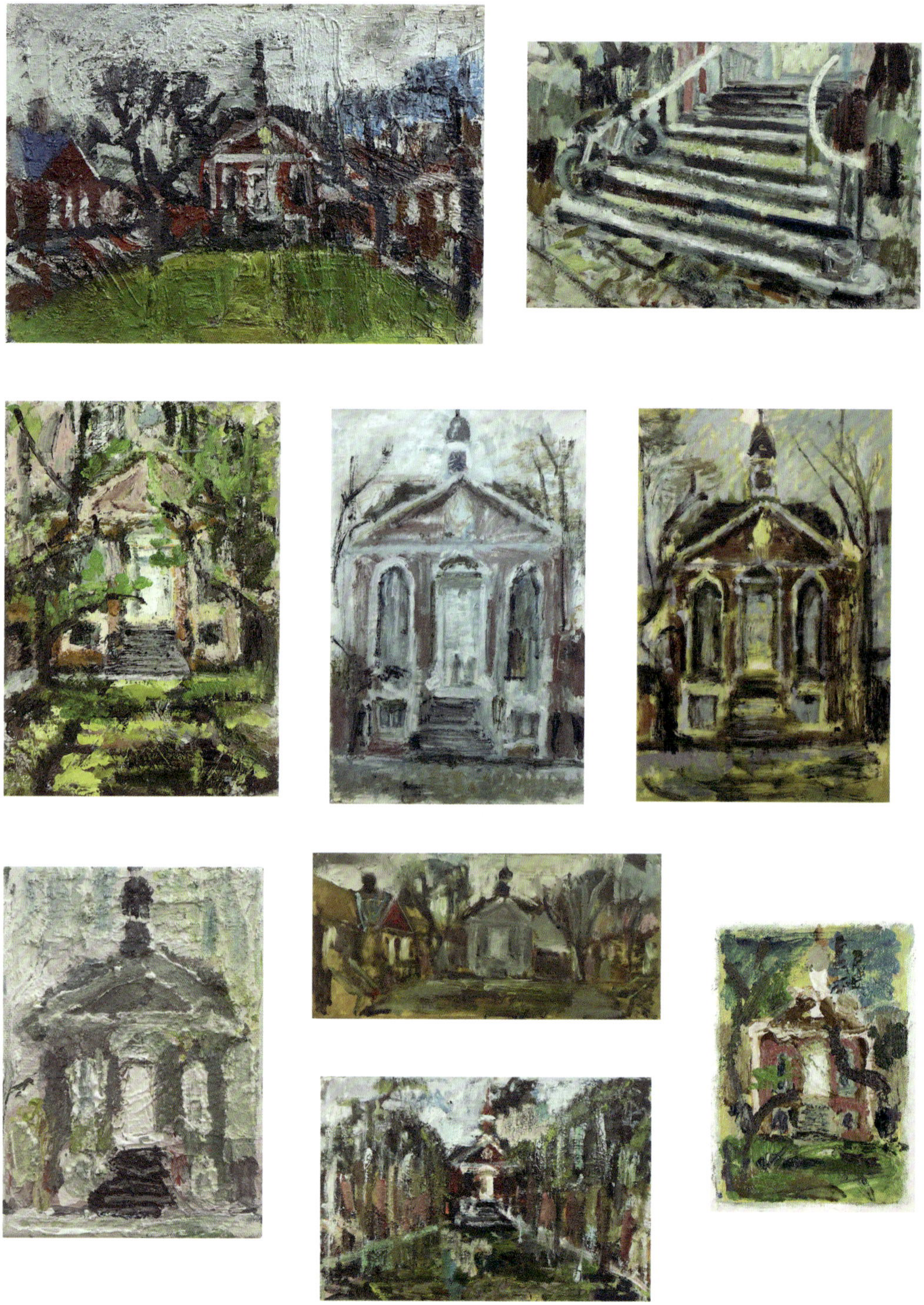

Trinity Green Chapel paintings, Grant Watson (2024)

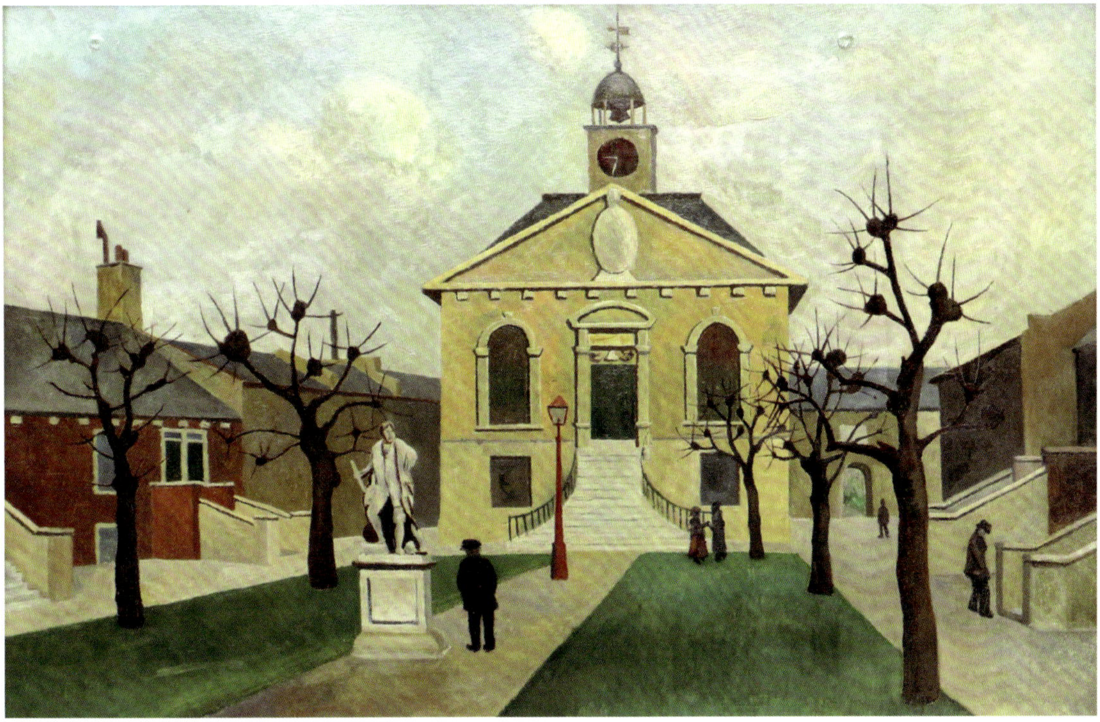

Almshouses, Mile End Road, Elwin Hawthorne (1935)
Elwin's notes reveal that this painting was sold from exhibition but was subsequently 'returned'. According to family history, this was the painting that was used to repair a shelf in his coal bunker!

09

Tate and Lyle Factory, Silvertown

Artist: Alex Pemberton
Medium: Oil on canvas
Dimensions: 76 x 107cm
Date: 2023

Views of the Thames have been subject matter in my work for more than twenty years, and my choice of Walter Steggles' painting of *Freighters in West India Dock* makes a clear link to this. The Tate and Lyle factory is a major landmark in the East End. It has been an important employer since it was first established in 1878, and a good subject for an exhibition about the East End. I am based in Greenwich and have painted the factory many times from the south shore. Other versions describe the alignment of buildings as a whole but did not convey its massive scale. In this piece I found that looking at a section of the facade helped to convey the scale of the place more directly. It was also a clearer way to describe the striking pattern it makes.

The whole thing might feel inhuman in its brashness, negating a human presence. Yet the idiosyncratic architecture, the history revealed in the piecemeal additions and the random assorted colours seem to show a human history, or some eccentric account of human progress – a colossal pattern arrived at by accident.

In making the painting I liked the angular forms this view presents, and the way one part was joined to another. It was like a frieze: a main frontal plane that was basically flat, with the roofs, silos and recesses for depth, and the pier and cranes projecting out in front of these.

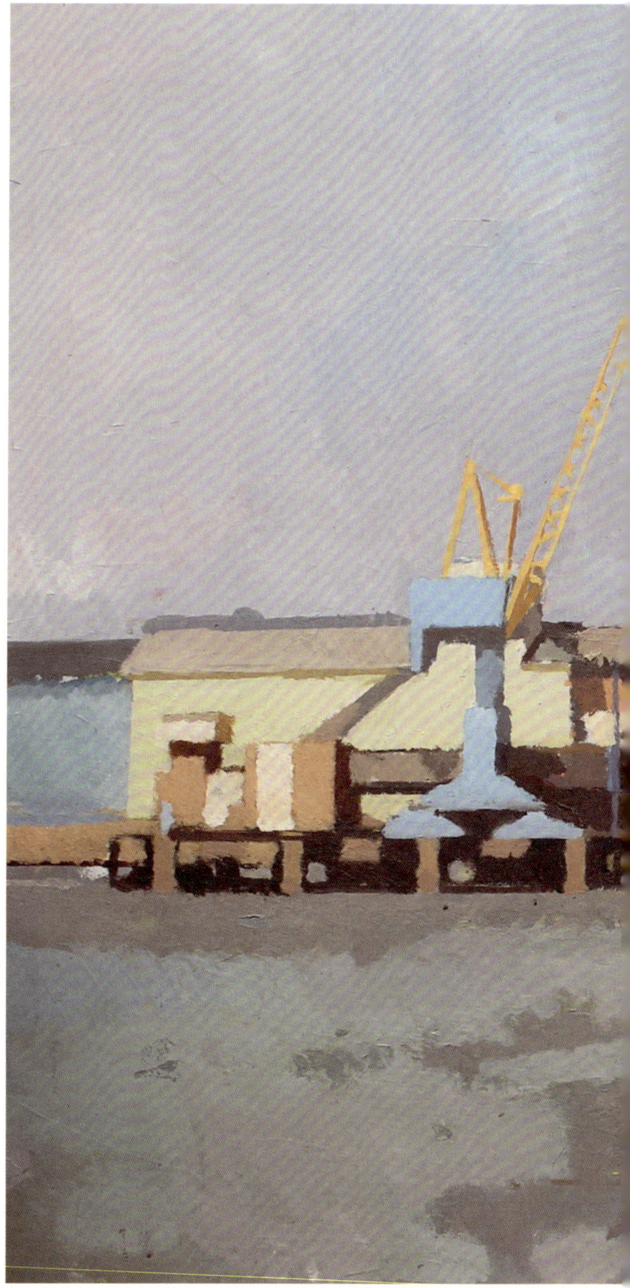

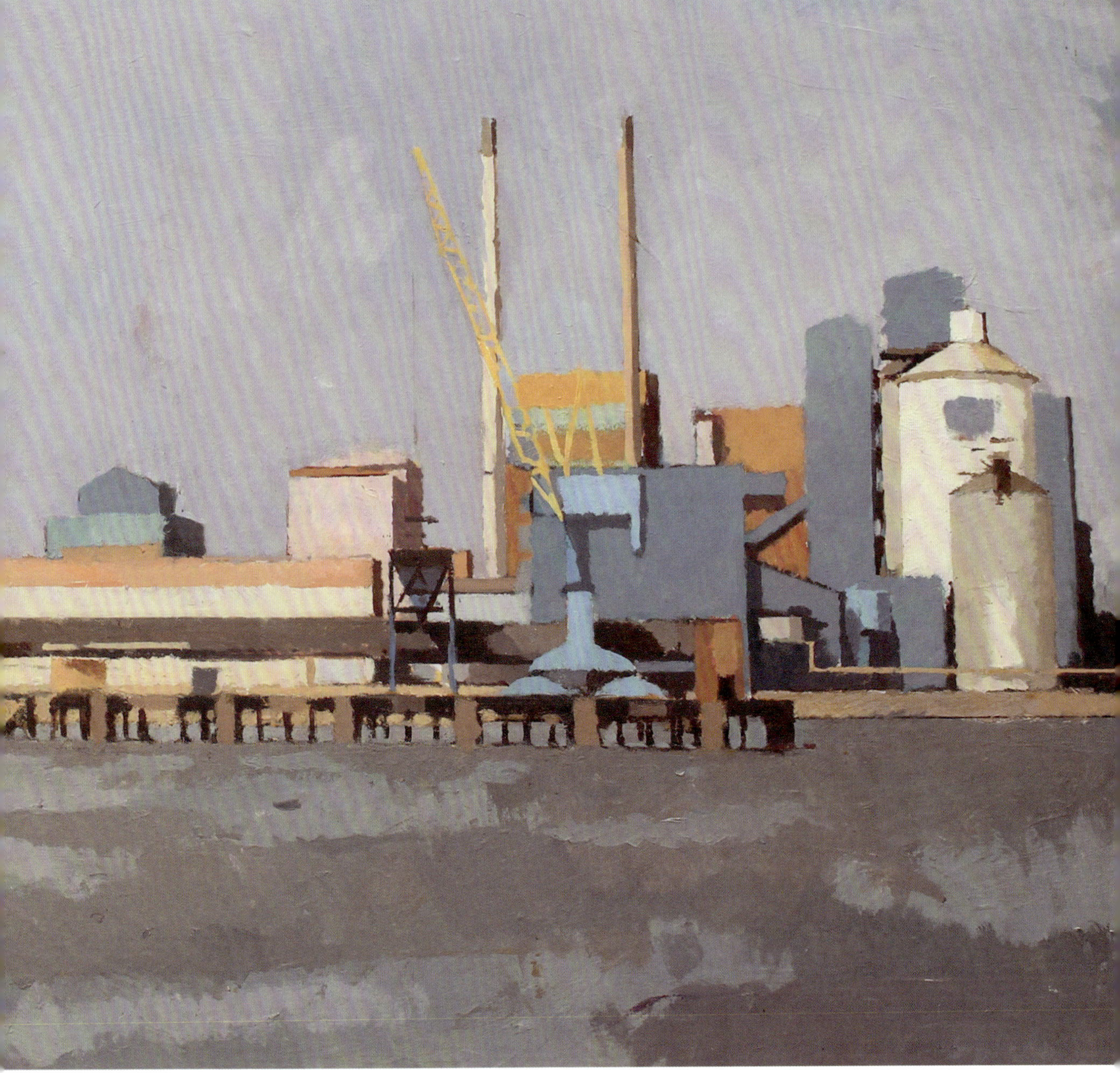

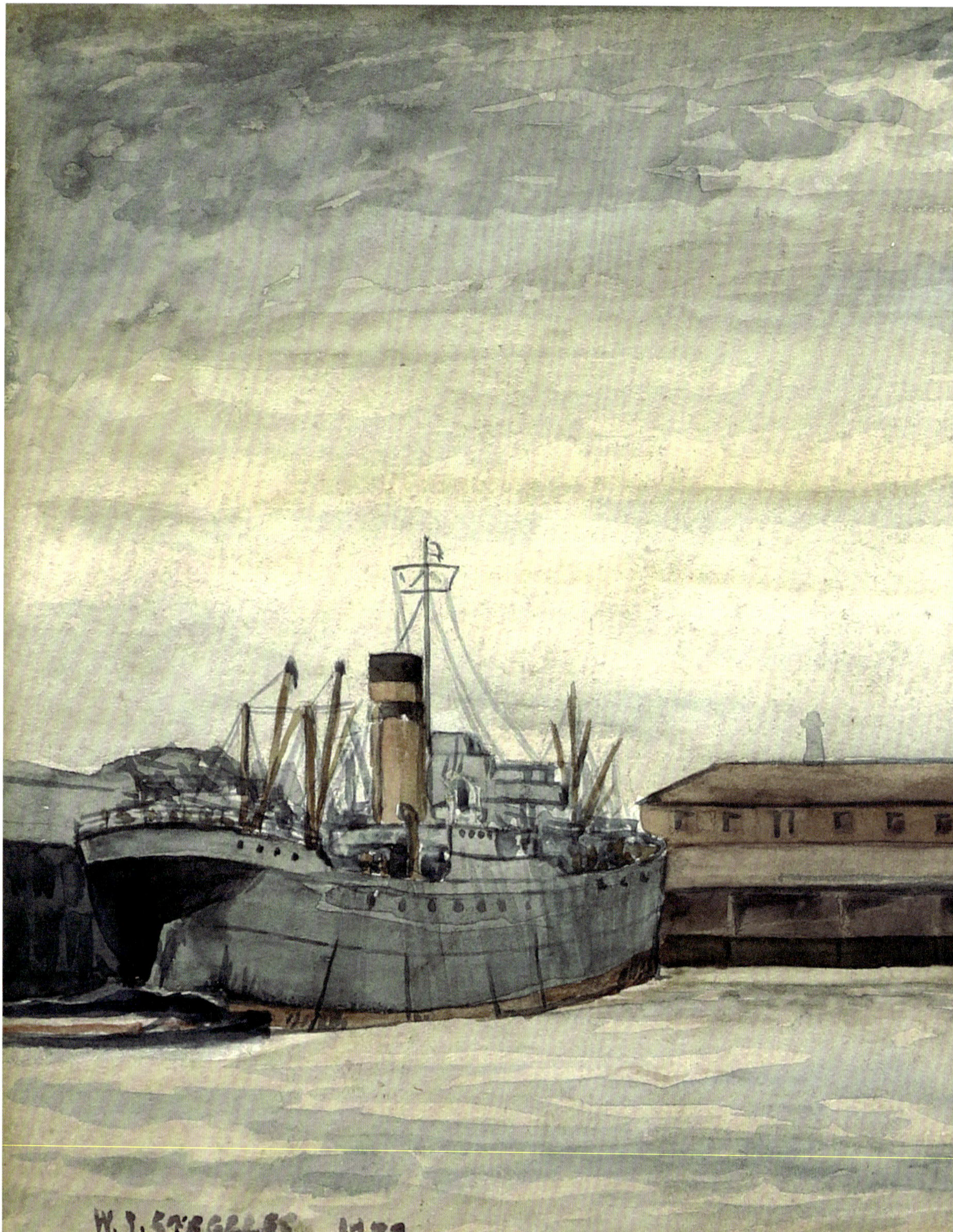
W. J. STEGGLES 1927

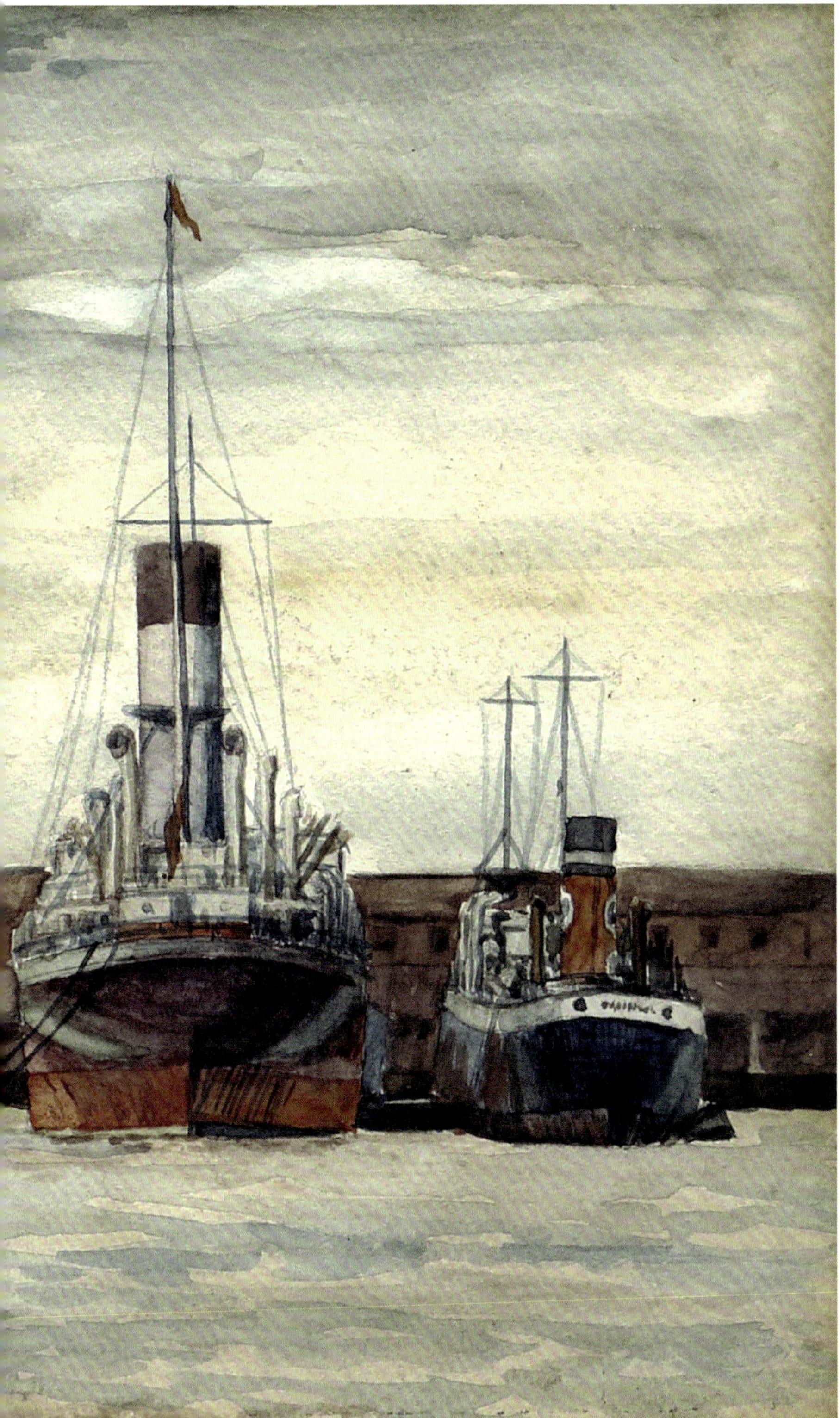

Freighters in West India Dock, Walter Steggles (1927)

Walter Steggles drew another version with the same title, which featured a tug called *Duncan* and a freighter called *Eula*. In this painting, the funnel colours of the three freighters might indicate that, from the left, the ships were owned by the Furness Withy Line, Blue Funnel Line and Blue Star Line. Walter worked for Furness Withy, which may explain his interest.

West India Dock (boundary between here and there)

Artist: Alexandra Blum

Medium: Watercolour on paper

Dimensions: 35 x 51cm

Date: 2024

I am fascinated by the industrial Thames and, after seeing Walter Steggles' *Freighters in West India Dock*, I was curious to see how the dock is used today. I discovered a hive of activity in place of the deserted dockside, austere warehouses and vast freighters that Steggles depicted.

I love the enduring calm Steggles created by eliminating movement in his image. However, when I was at the dockside, painting from direct observation, the dynamic spatial layers and the events unfolding around them were the aspects I found exhilarating. I focused on discovering the landscape gradually, rather than in a single glance, mentally travelling between forms, as if they were stepping stones leading me in small increments around the dock. I wanted the tumult of the entire

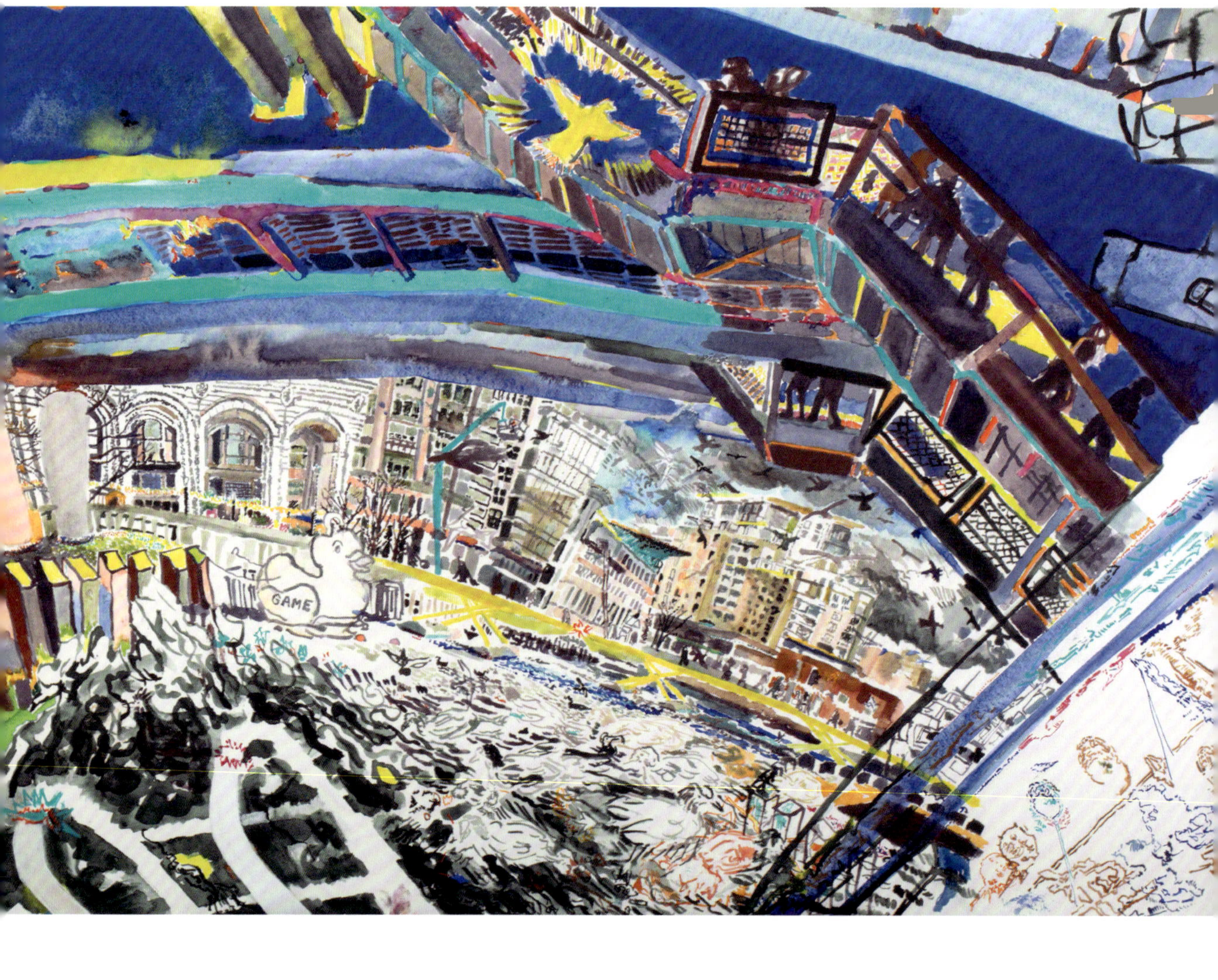

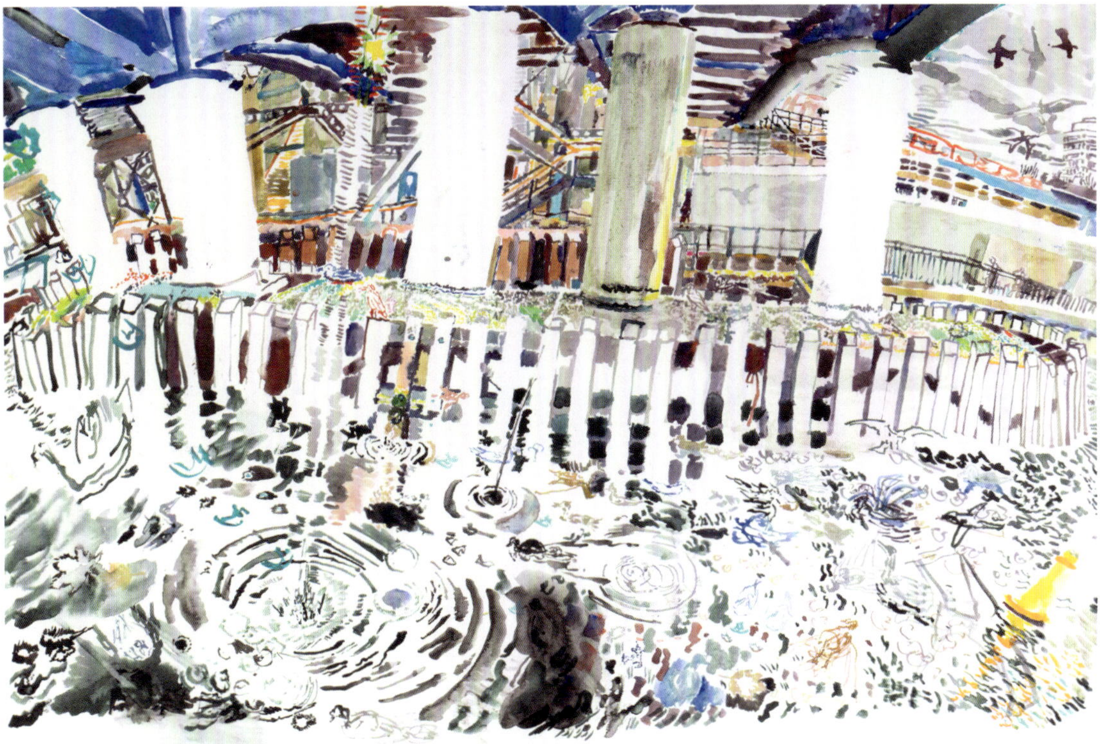

West India Dock (North Dock), Alexandra Blum (2024)

space to emerge out of an accumulation of the minutiae I noticed, in order to record the ceaseless interactions taking place between urban structures, water formations, and human and non-human life.

At the docks, old warehouses, cranes and wooden dockside walls can still be seen alongside the contemporary infrastructure – reminders of the area's dark history as a dock that was integral to the brutal exploitation of enslaved people, colonial exploitation, and the poor working conditions of dock labourers. As I painted, I felt privileged to be able to spend time looking closely at the spatial rhythms and life currently taking place, investigating and recording through both mark and colour.

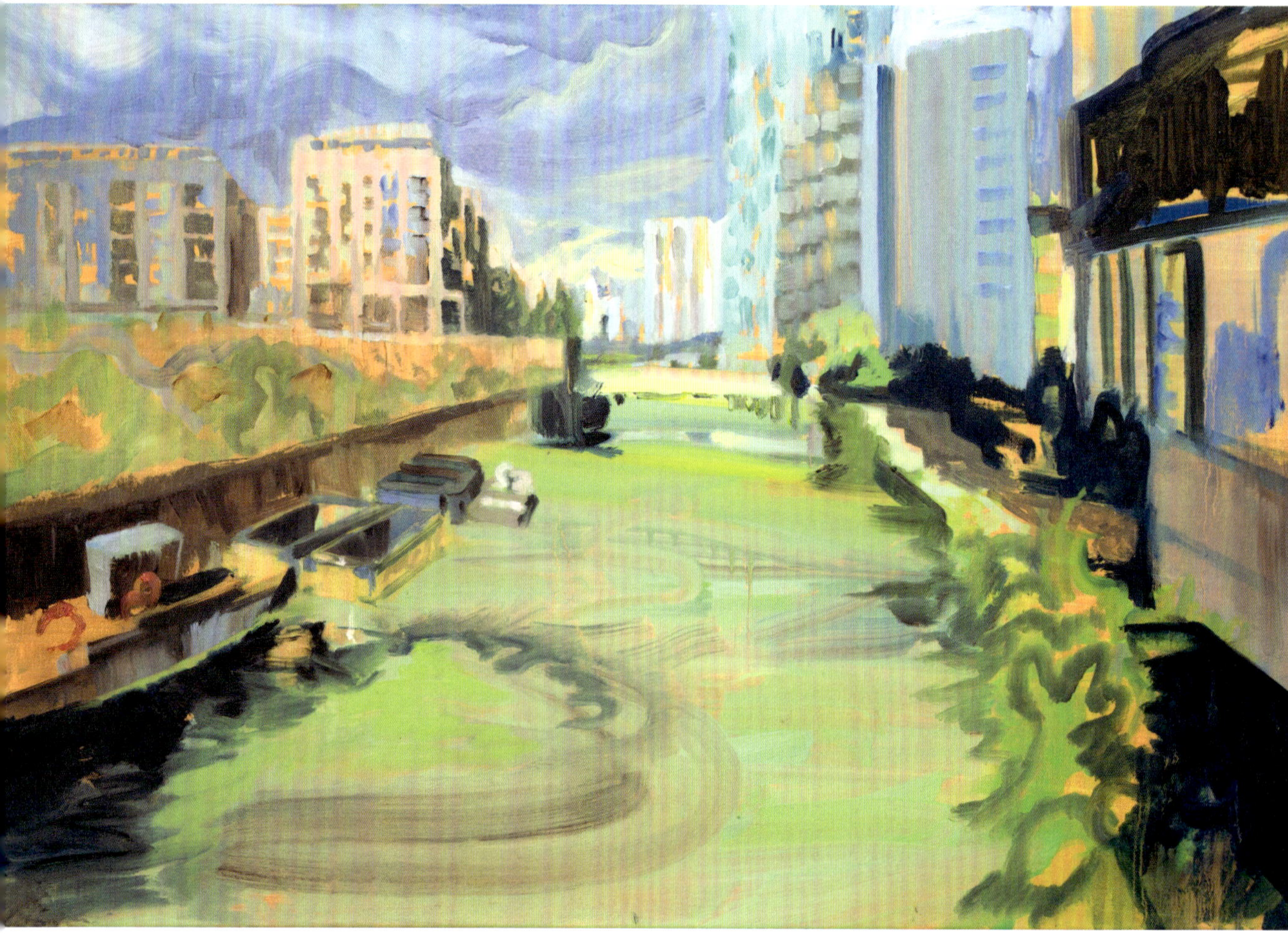

11

Bow Back Rivers Algae Bloom

Artist: Fiona McIntyre

Medium: Oil on linen

Dimensions: 51 x 76cm

Date: 2024

I visited Bow Back Rivers in the East End of London in early September 2023 and responded to the colour contrasts and patterns of modern high-rise buildings against the scrubland. Luminous algae blooms in the water were lit up in lime-coloured stripes by the late summer sun. My inspiration was Walter Steggles and his depiction of *Red Bridge* in the London industrial backwaters. The light in his paintings is clearly influenced by London smog, which was a dirty yellow-green colour. My painting is a modern version, because although London smog is a thing of the past, we are instead contending with the pollution of our waterways and aquatic life.

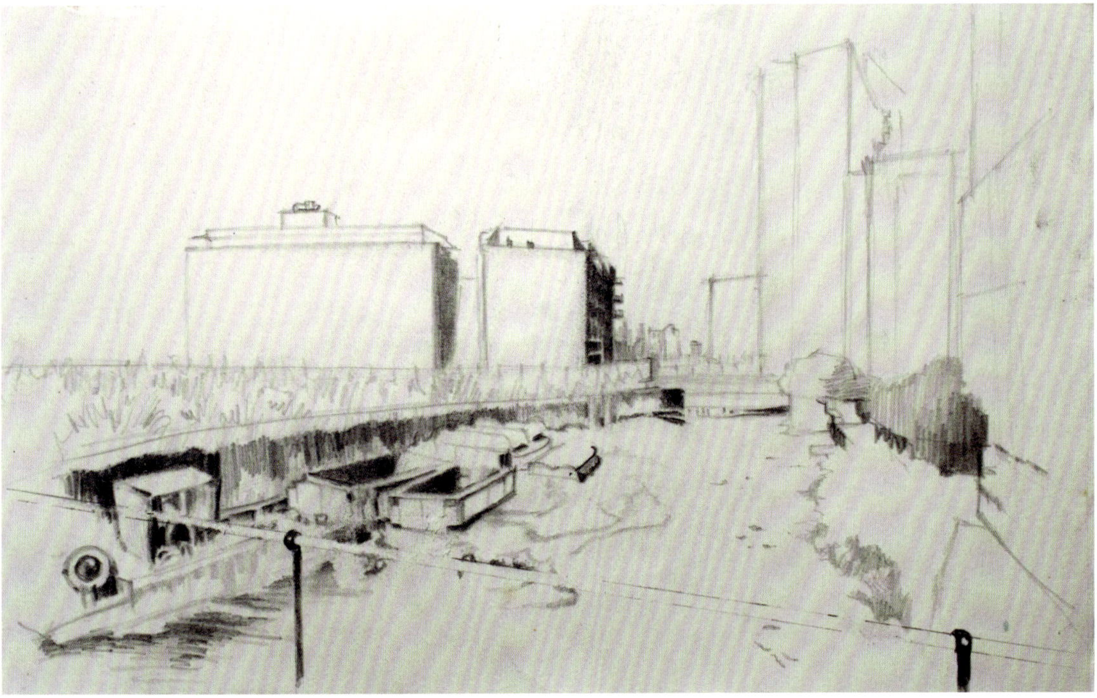

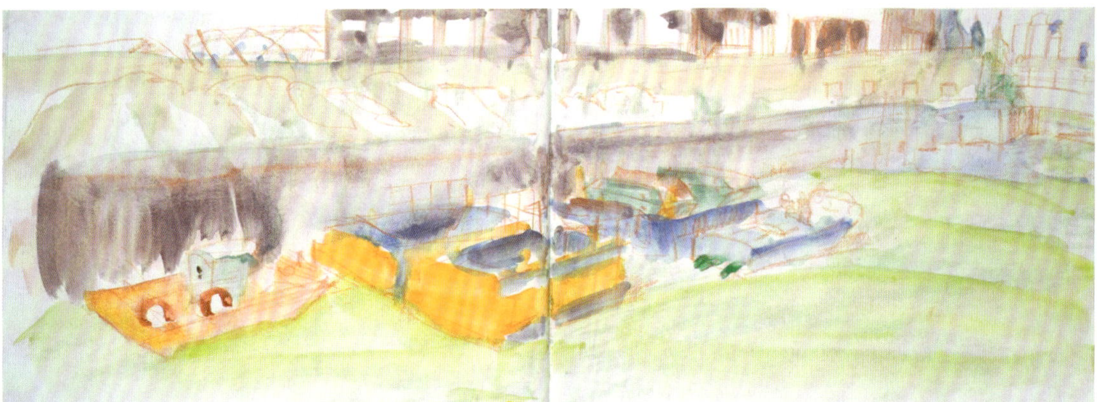

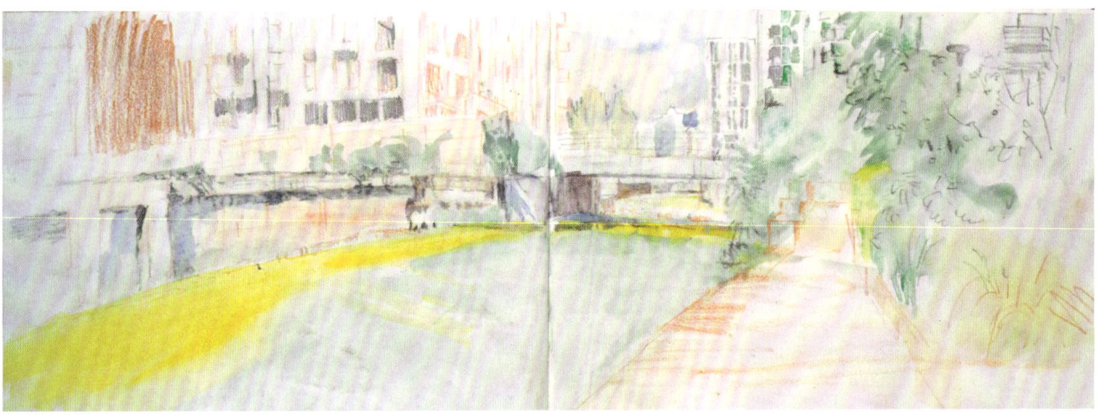

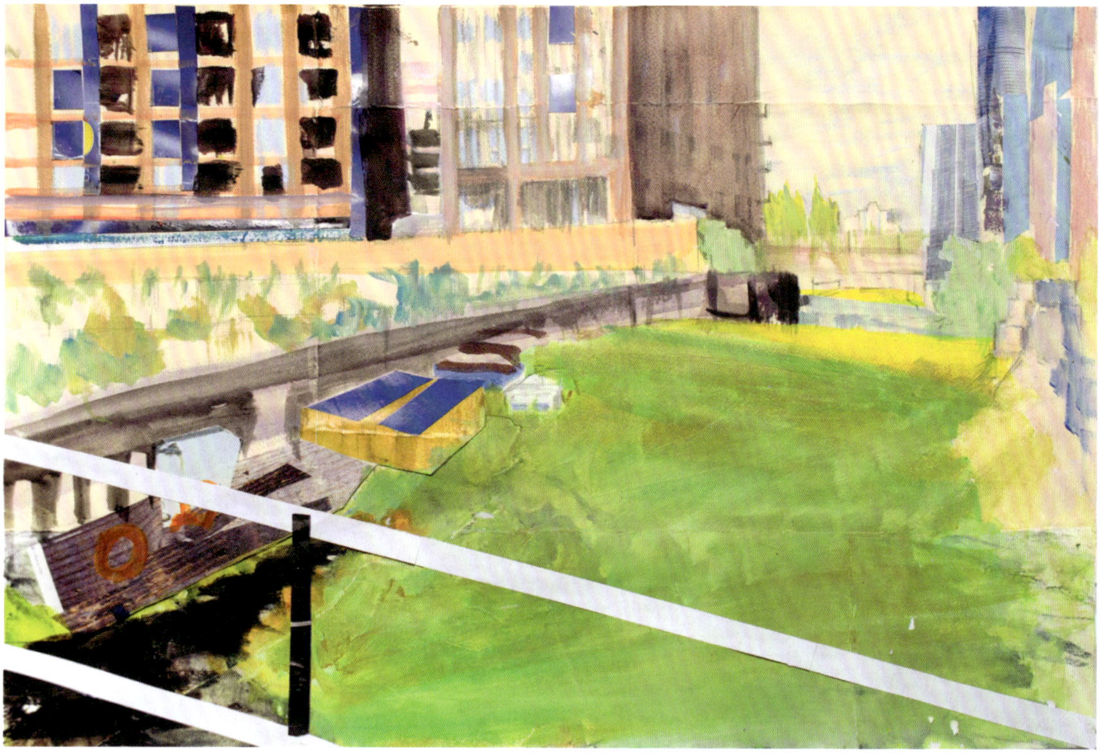

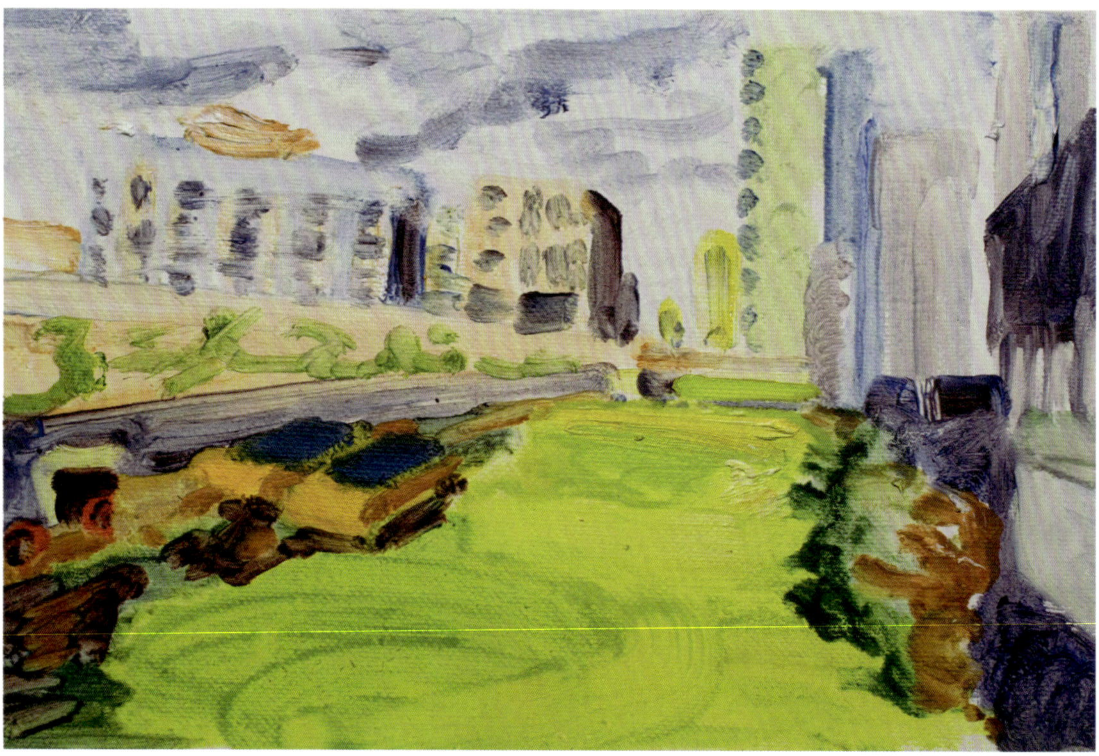

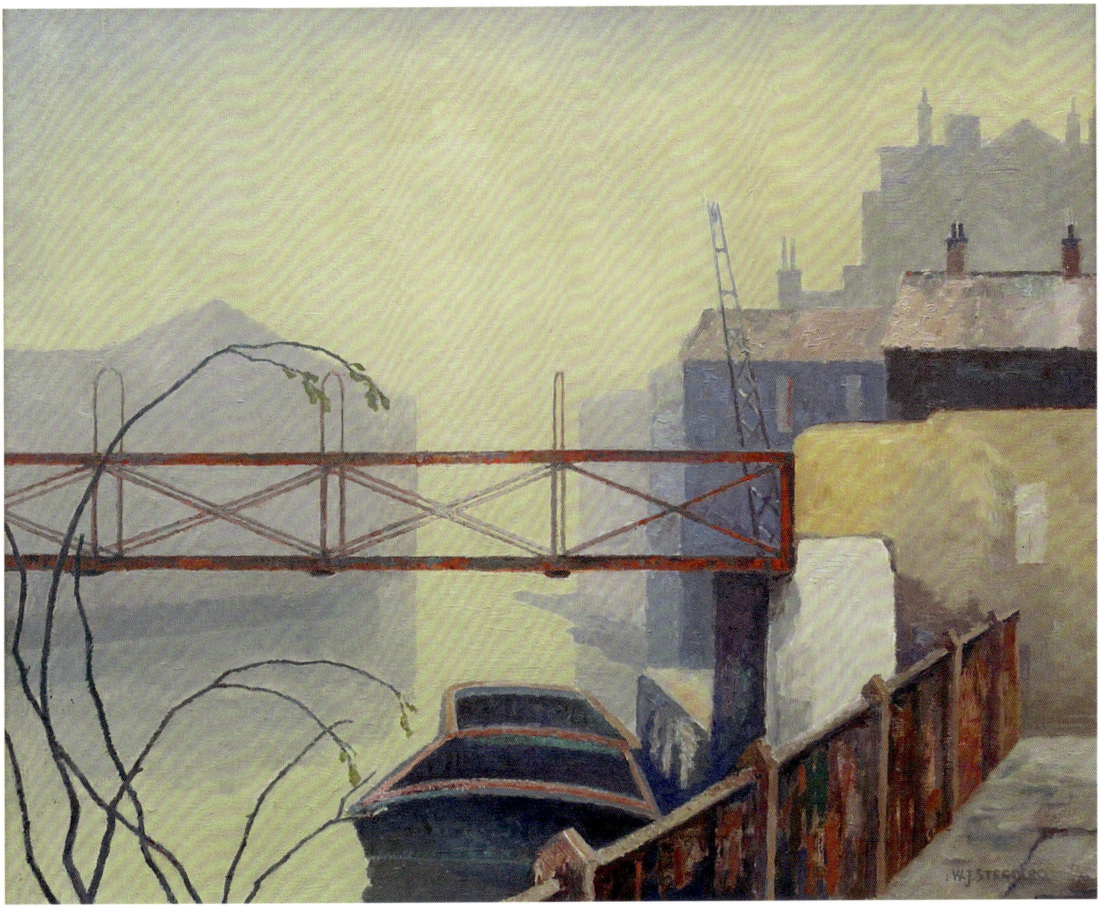

Red Bridge, Walter Steggles (undated)

Although this painting most likely dates from the 1960s, it was based on a series of sketches that Walter Steggles made in 1931. The footbridge in the painting was near the old Bryant and May factory, allowing their workers from Stratford to easily cross the Lea Navigation to get to work. Walter also utilized the bridge as his viewpoint for *Five Bells Wharf* and *Canal at Bow*, both of which date from 1931.

12

After Harold Steggles, Memories St Mark's Church and Mare Street

Artist: Philippa Beale

Medium: Mixed media on canvas

Dimensions: 92 x 112cm

Date: 2024

Recreating the past is always a complex and challenging task, and to recall any particular period in history requires significant effort and imagination. Construction, revamping and remodelling over the last forty years has been so comprehensive that the street where I used to have my studio, and the different sites of Central Saint Martins, where I taught, are now unrecognizable. So many community buildings have been converted – 'repurposed', in the modern phrase – into expensive living accommodations, designer outlets or chic coffee houses; the latter having perhaps more of a historical echo with the area.

The culture of providing East End inhabitants with vocational training has almost disappeared. The School of Fashion survives, but the printers, shoe designers and leather workers are no longer there. The Cordwainers School closed and was asset-stripped more than twenty years ago; the only reminder of that centuries-old tradition of shoe manufacturing and the area's equally old European connections is a bronze statue in Watling Street.

To re-recognize those parts of the East End that were central to my life, I looked at what were for me relevant and iconic buildings, each time with three aims. One, to conjure up the shop where my husband's relatives sold tinware (they were probably refugees from Eastern Europe escaping religious persecution). Two, to look at the locations where I taught and managed two sites, dodging daily between each building amid the then congested traffic. Three, to include one thing that has not and will never change: the continued survival of the city's flora and fauna, which pops up out of the cracks in the pavements and nests in every nook and cranny.

What has happened in the East End has happened all over England in the last twenty-five years: there is no individuality, quaintness or charm. What do remain are the churches, and after executing several small research paintings, I selected *St Mark's Church* by Harold Steggles as inspiration. Like residents of the 'new East End', I am forced to rely on imaginative memory, for to paint what the Steggles brothers painted when they were part of the East London Group is an impossibility. Their world no longer exists.

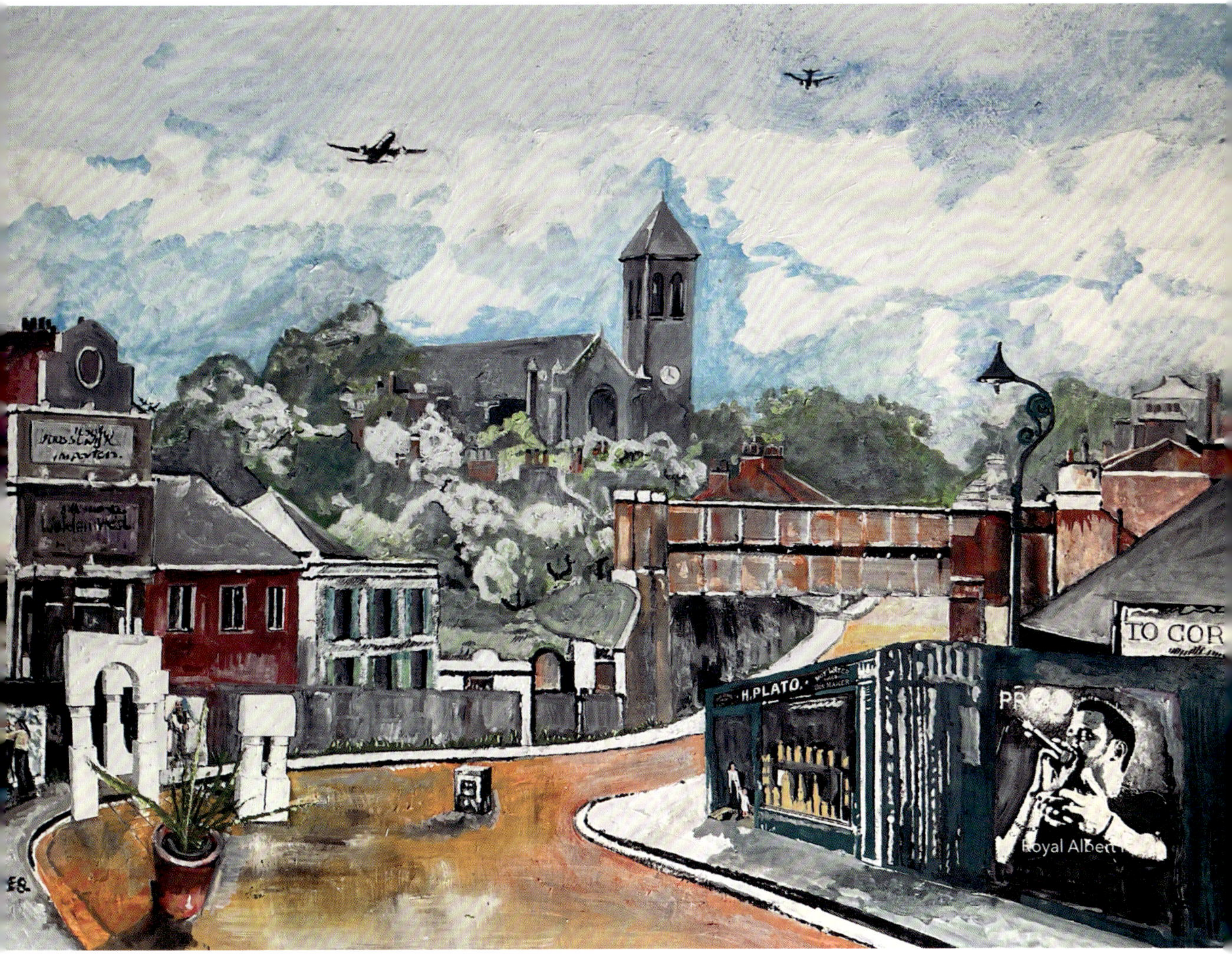
H. PLATO.
TO COR

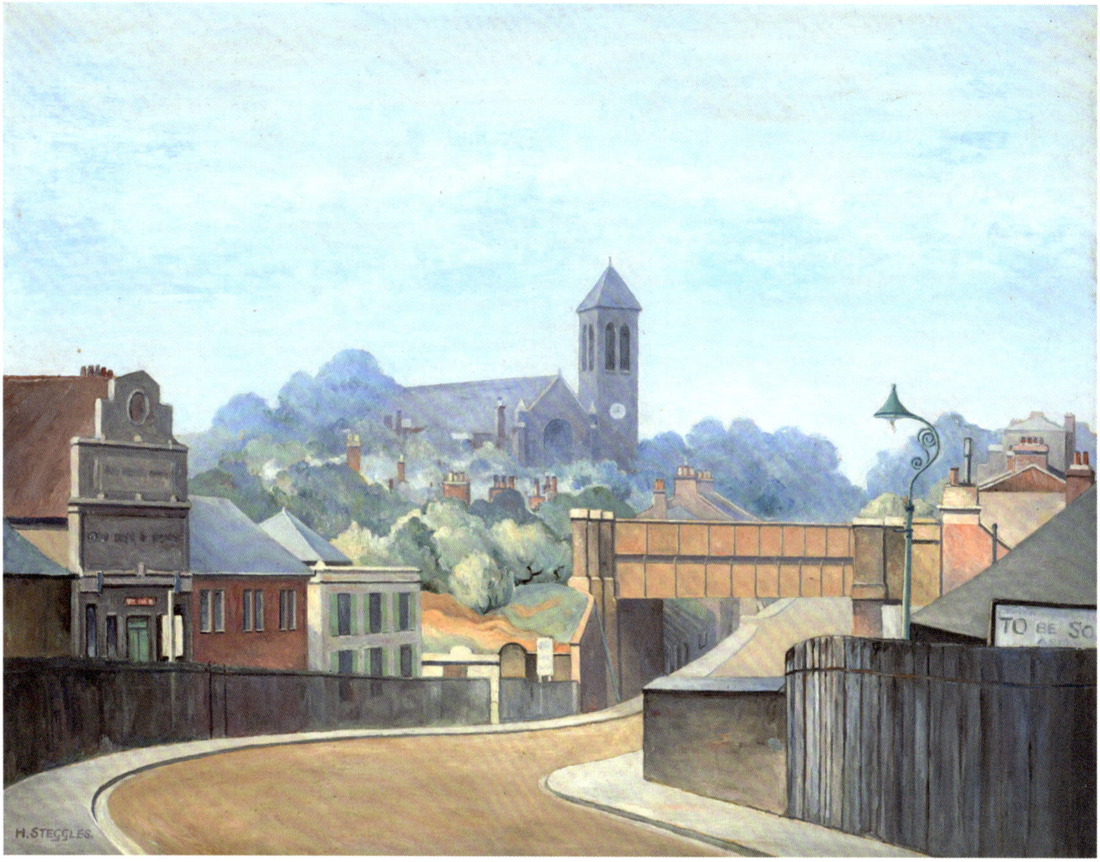

St Mark's Church, Harold Steggles (1932)

This view of St Mark's Church (in Victoria Park) was taken from Wick Lane, at a point near 1–4 Wick Lane. The large building in the foreground to the left is the Public Baths.

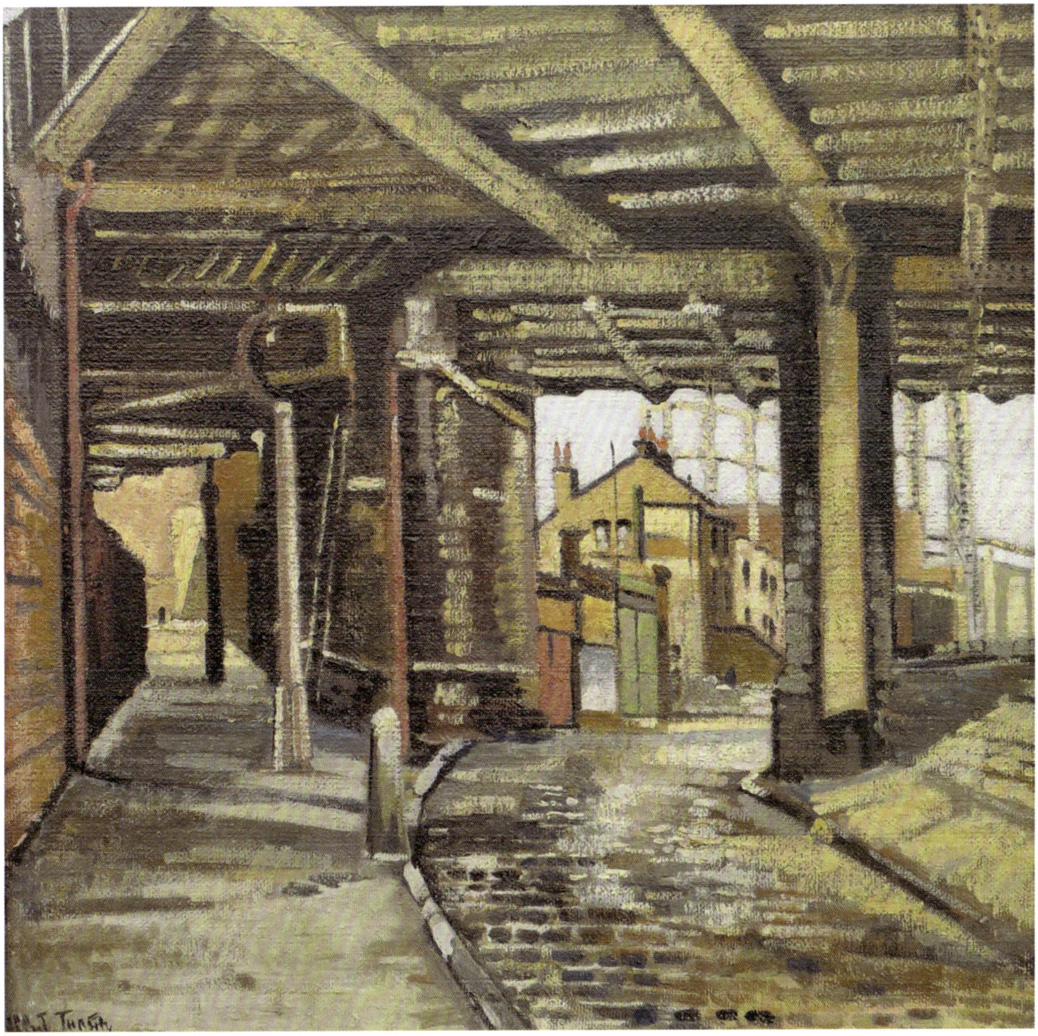

The Arches, Cambridge Heath Road, Albert Turpin (undated)

In his later life, Albert set himself the task of capturing as much of the rapidly disappearing parts of his beloved Bethnal Green as he could. This view was taken from Corbridge Crescent, looking towards the gasholders of what was originally the Imperial Gas Light and Coke Company's site, with the old Empress Coach Company premises to the left.

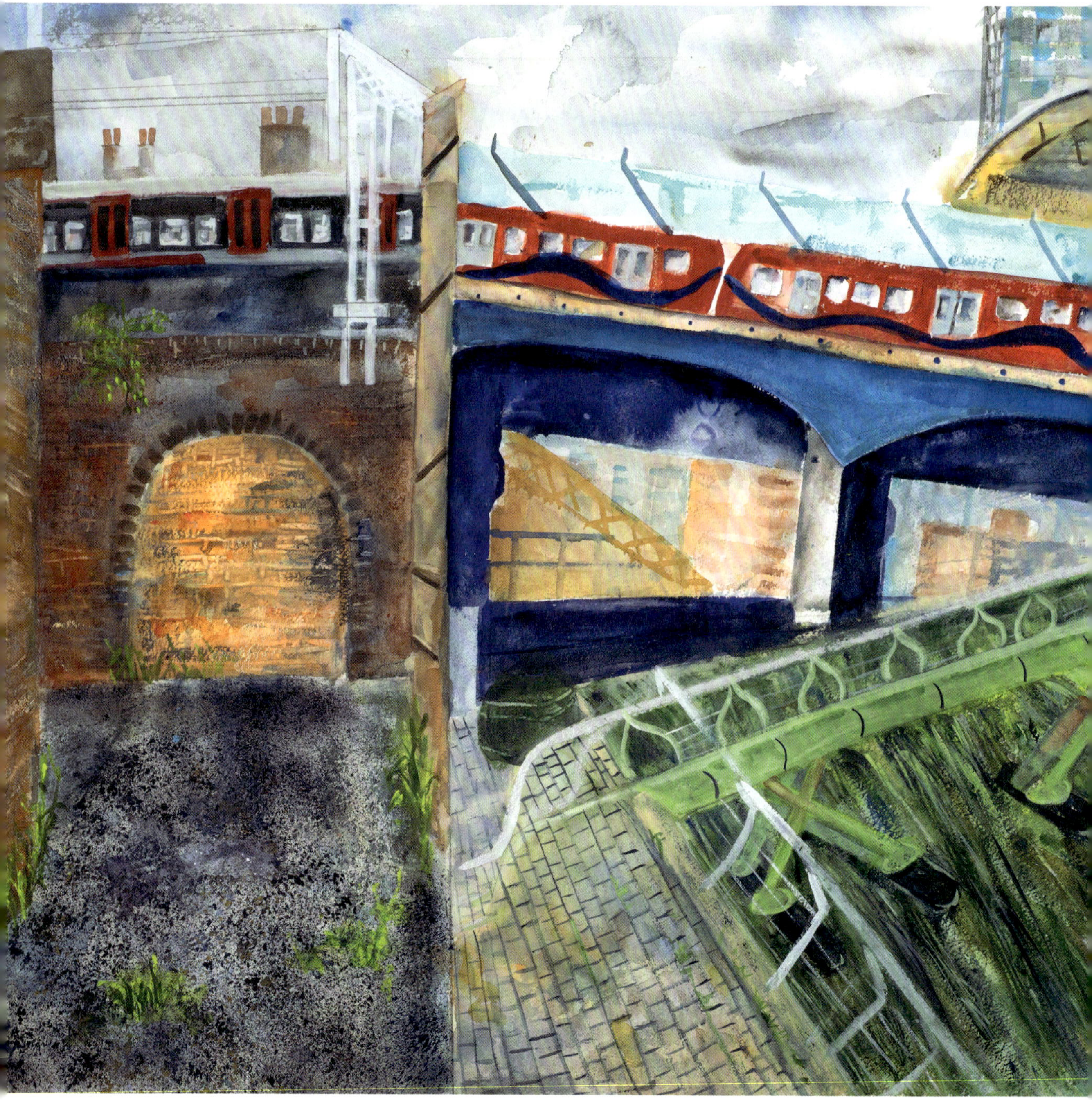

13

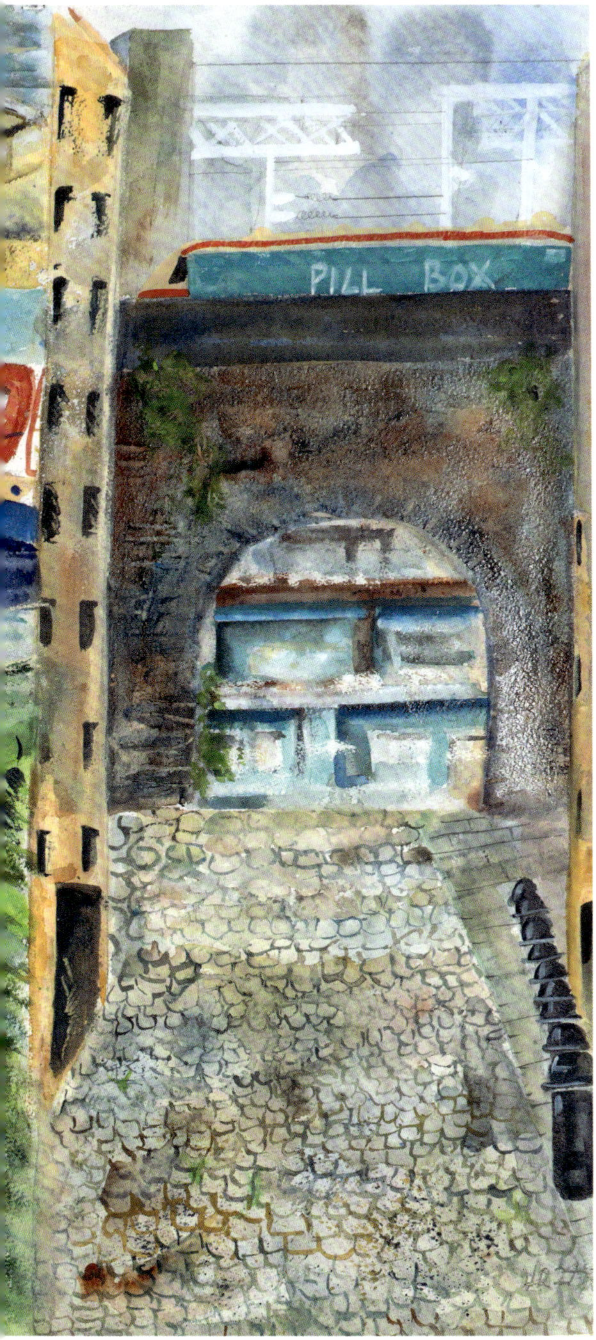

Bethnal Green and East India Docklands (Triptych)

Artist: Hilary Rosen
Medium: Watercolour and gouache
Dimensions: 100 × 65cm
Date: 2024

I often spent days in Bethnal Green as a child, as my father's cousins lived in a prefab there and knew the Krays.

Having been brought up in the centre of London, I have often been inspired by cityscapes. While at art school I made images of urban architecture, which is still one of the main sources of inspiration for my work. Albert Turpin's *The Arches, Cambridge Heath Road* was an inspiration for my triptych in watercolour and gouache. I made in situ drawings in pencil and in water-based oil pastels of two derelict arches and their surrounds on Cambridge Heath Road – the same street that inspired Albert Turpin.

The other inspirational painting was *Freighters in West India Dock* by Walter Steggles. Here I sketched in situ the juxtaposition of the old wharf buildings with the contemporary architecture of finance buildings and offices, the Thames, the bridges and Docklands Light Railway.

Each part of my image features a train running through it, connecting the elements of my triptych, but also acting as a metaphor for connecting different parts of East London, with flashes of bright colour in contrast to the monotone but textured architecture.

I was delighted to be asked to exhibit in this show, as the subject matter and the ethos of the ELG is something I find inspiring and innovative – plus I teach painting in adult education classes.

14

Austerity, Dehumanisation, Disappearance

Artist: Nicole Poh

Medium: Acrylic on canvas

Dimensions: 100 × 70cm

Date: 2023

During one of my walks in the East London area, I came across a construction project involving the demolition of Robin Hood Gardens. This project aims to replace the demolished structure with four blocks of tenure homes, accompanied by an external landscaped area.

Inquisitive about the rationale behind the demolition of Robin Hood Gardens, I discovered that it was a significant example of Brutalist architecture. The experience created a sense of nostalgia and contemplation of the changing cityscape and the consequences of urbanization.

Brutalism is widely recognized as having produced some of the most visually impactful designs of the twentieth century. However, the achievement of the structure was considered both astounding and contentious due to the utilization of unfinished concrete for its exterior surfaces, hence necessitating its demolition.

My current paintings are investigating the implications of the materials utilized in these buildings and their impact on society. Specifically, I am interested in understanding the consequences of discontinuing the use of these materials and exploring methods for their retention or preservation.

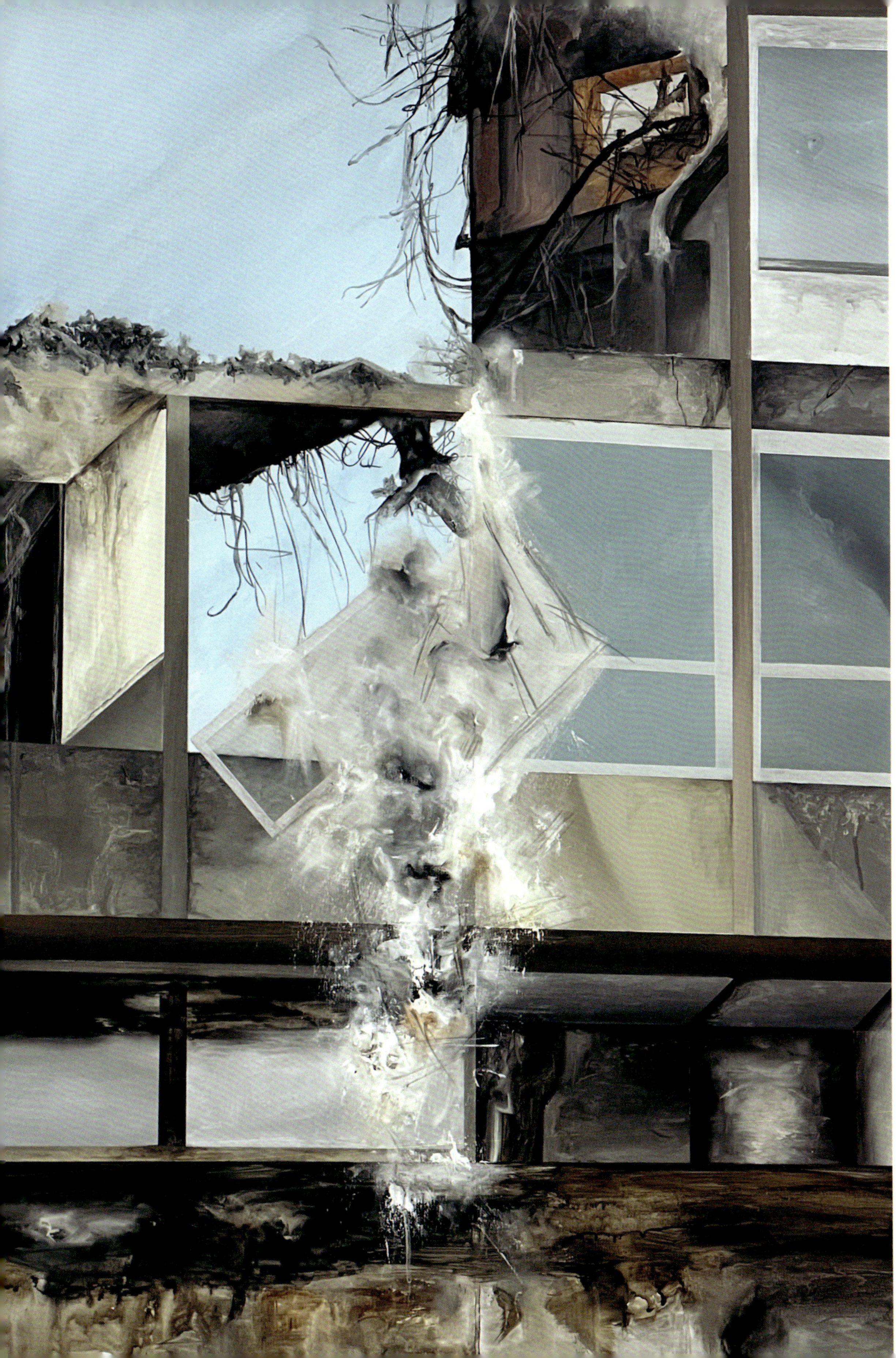

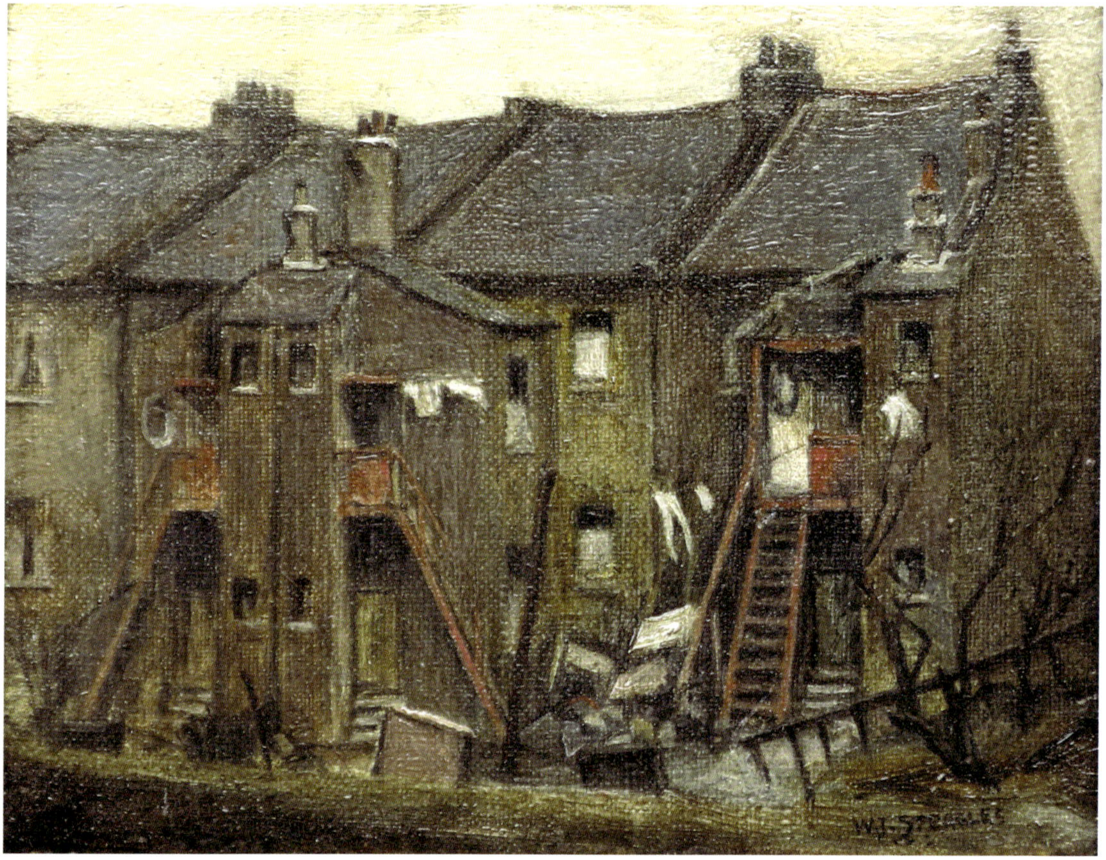

Old Houses, Bethnal Green, Walter Steggles (1930)

This is a fascinating little painting on several levels, depicting as it does the harsh reality of day-to-day life for so many East Enders at the time. Sadly, the precise location of the painting is unknown but it seems very likely that it could have been a view from a window at one of the evening art class locations. Intriguingly, although Walter lists it in his studio book as being completed in 1930, it featured in an article in *Creative Arts* magazine in August 1929.

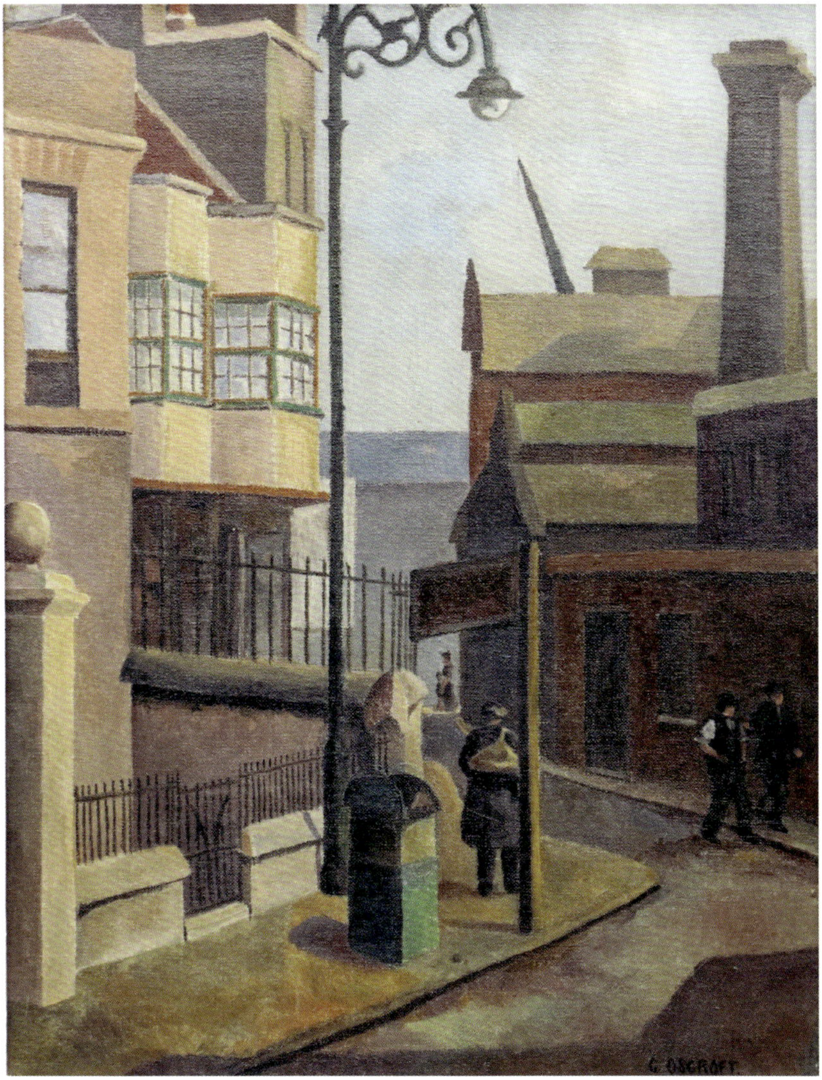

Old Houses, Bow, Grace Oscroft (1934)

Dating from 1934, this painting was shown at Alex Reid & Lefevre Galleries in their 'British & French Artists' exhibition in 1935. The scene depicts a view of 223 Bow Road, a corn and flour dealer's business run by Thomas Howes, whose ancestor had established the business in 1818. The building has had numerous reincarnations in recent years but is still there, despite dating from the seventeenth century!

15

View of Canonbury Tower, Summer 2023

Inspired both by Harold Steggles' painting of Canonbury Tower in 1938 and the fact that I have lived in Islington for nearly four decades, I chose to paint this view on a summer's day. It is an interesting building and a lovely area, and I enjoyed standing painting on a street corner, bumping into several old friends and neighbours and reminiscing about drunken and sober times on that road.

Artist: Melissa Scott-Miller

Medium: Oil on canvas

Dimensions: 50 × 60cm

Date: 2023

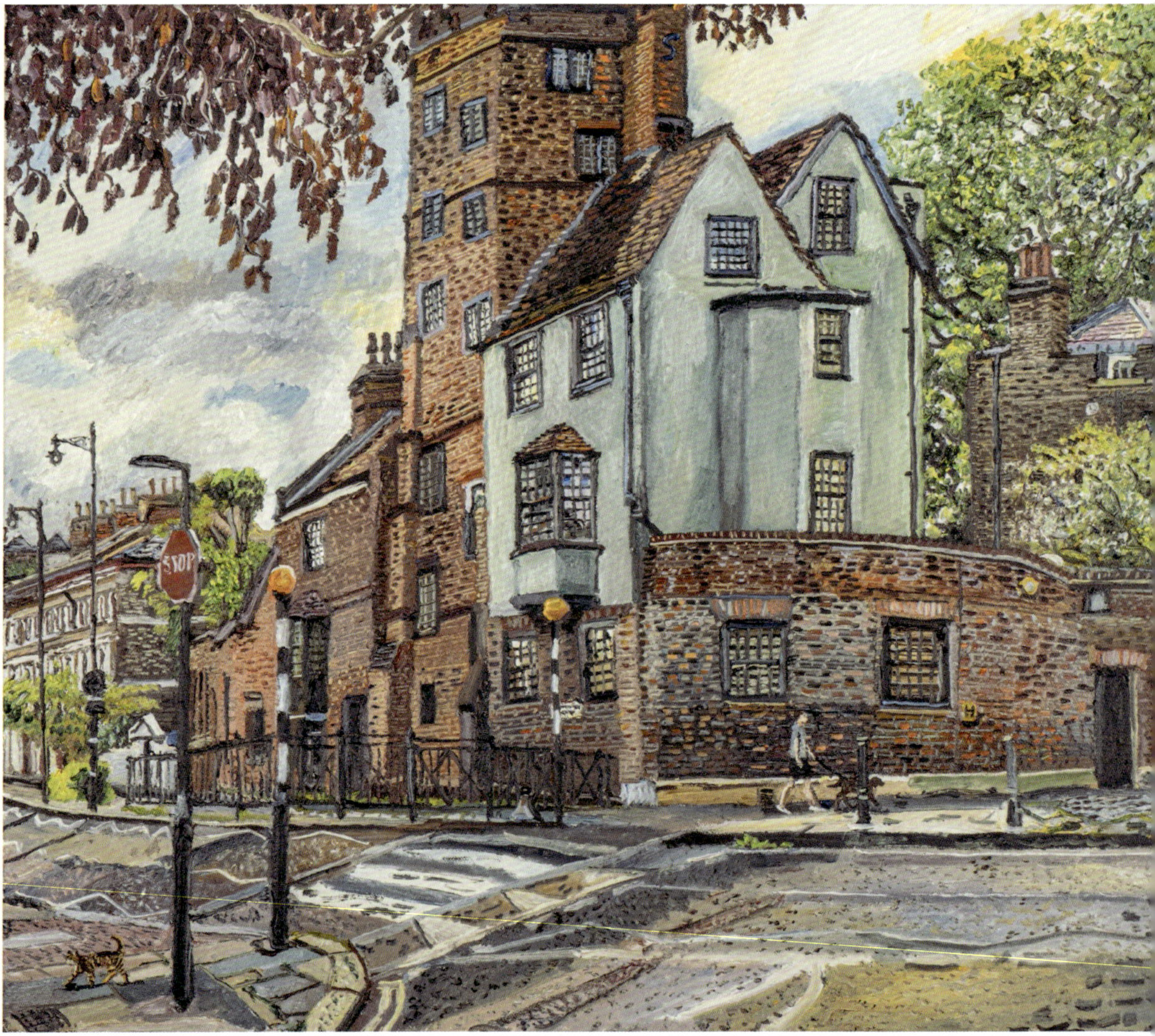

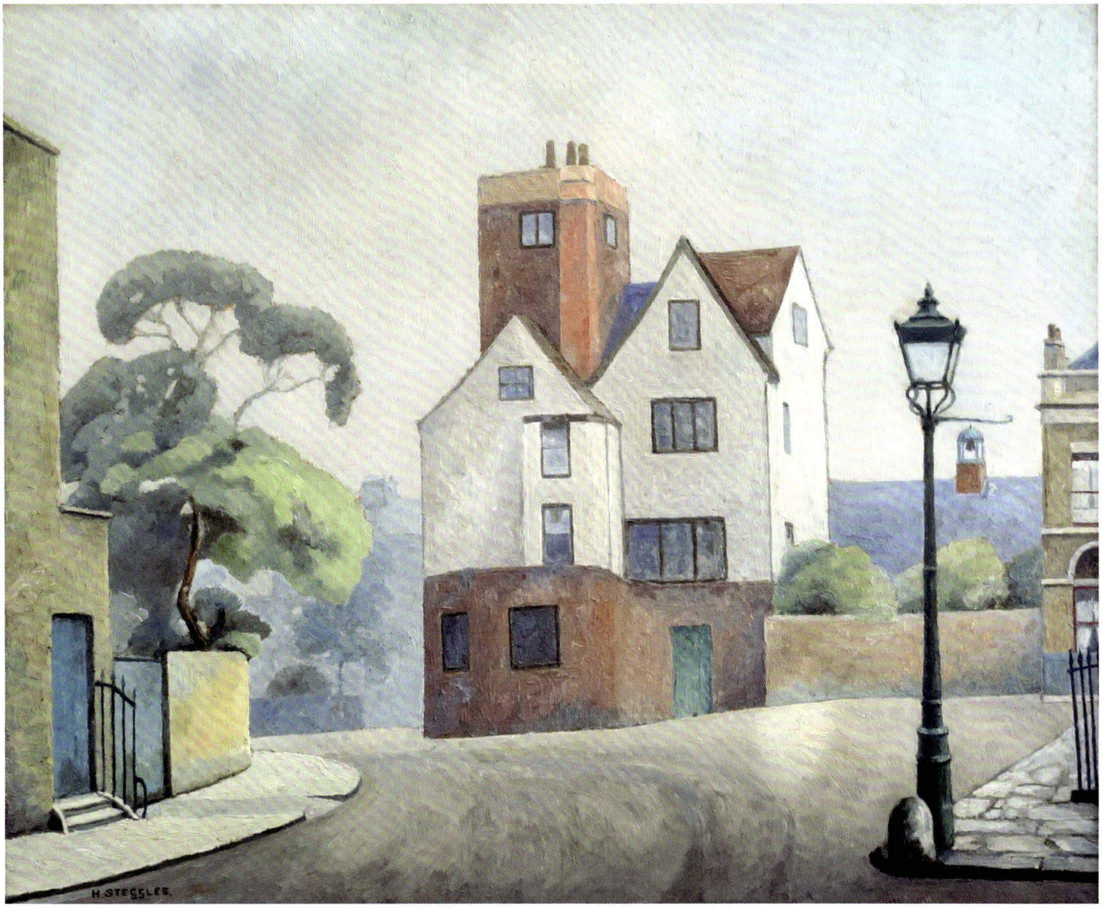

Canonbury, Harold Steggles (1938)

Quite how Harold came to paint this view is a bit of a mystery because there's little evidence of him painting anywhere else nearby. It is possible that he might have been inspired by Elwin Hawthorne, who painted in the area in 1932, 1933 and 1934. In 1940, Harold gave the painting to his younger sister, Phyllis, as a wedding present.

16

Under Canonbury Tower

Artist: Timothy Hyman, R.A.
Medium: Oil on canvas
Dimensions: 110 x 60cm
Date: 2023/24

Canonbury Tower is a Tudor oddity – a landmark but an anomaly in its setting of nineteenth-century terraces. I live within walking distance and have always felt some uplift in its emanation – as I generally do with towers! But the painting developed unexpectedly over a period when my soulmate fell in the street and suddenly died in hospital. Her Parkinsonian forward-thrusting figure took the place of a previously anonymous passer-by. Even before that, I'd found the planet Saturn also intruding at top right. A friend who photographed me at the tower (art historian Paul Hills) suggested it somehow resembled me – awkward, tall and unstable.

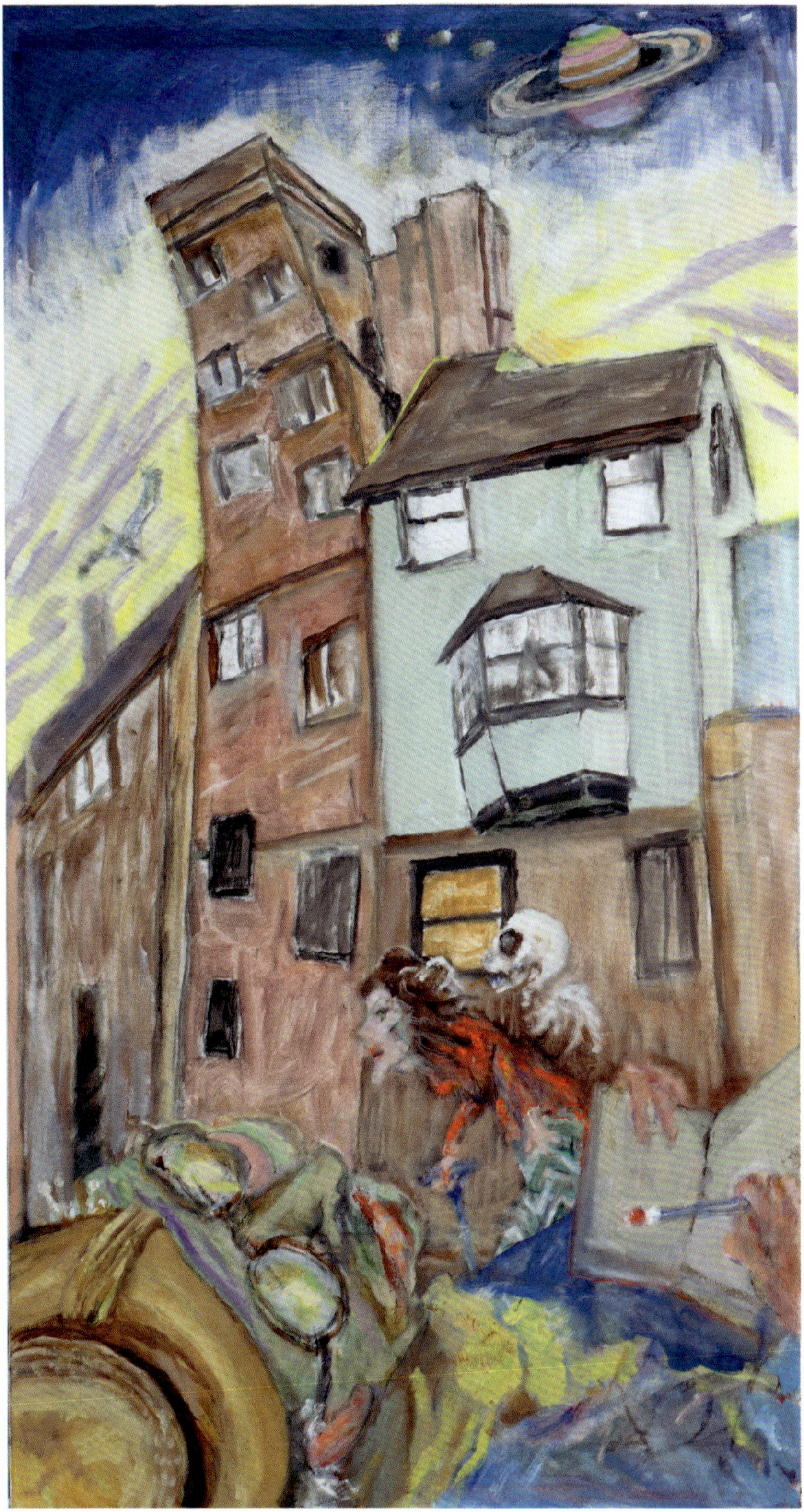

17

Regent's Canal (Grove Road)

Artist: Tim Craven
Medium: Watercolour and body colour
Dimensions: 57 x 67cm
Date: 2024

The East London Group was a sort of junior cousin of the London Group to which I was elected a member in 2015, but it failed to survive World War II as it lacked a sustainable infrastructure. As Curator of Art at Southampton City Art Gallery, I was instrumental in staging an ELG exhibition there in 2017 (following a London Group centenary exhibition in 2014). With such associations and my accumulated art historical knowledge, I was delighted to participate in this project. I explored the Grove Road area for a subject and found my favourite on the nearby canal – a combination of diverse visual delights.

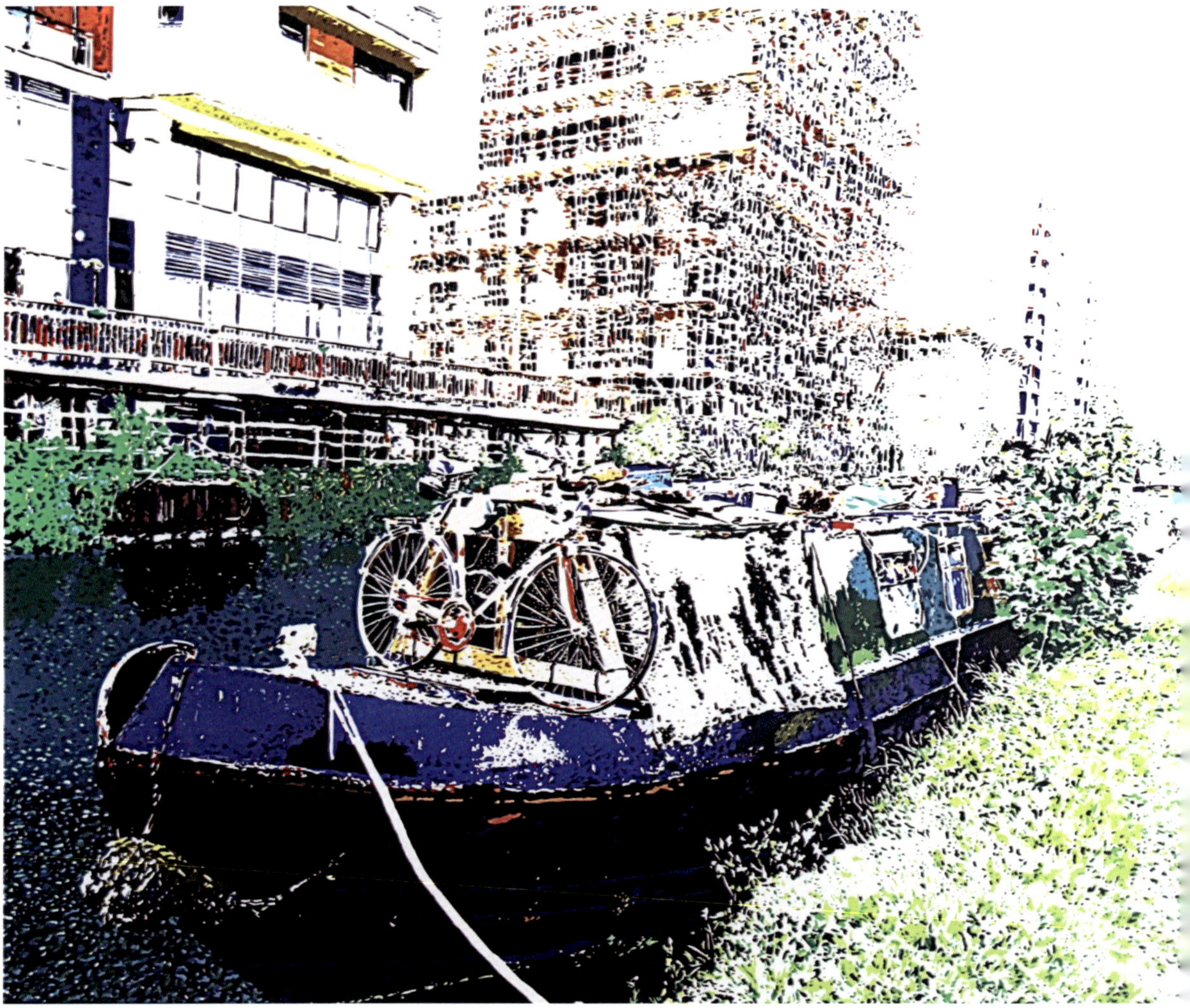

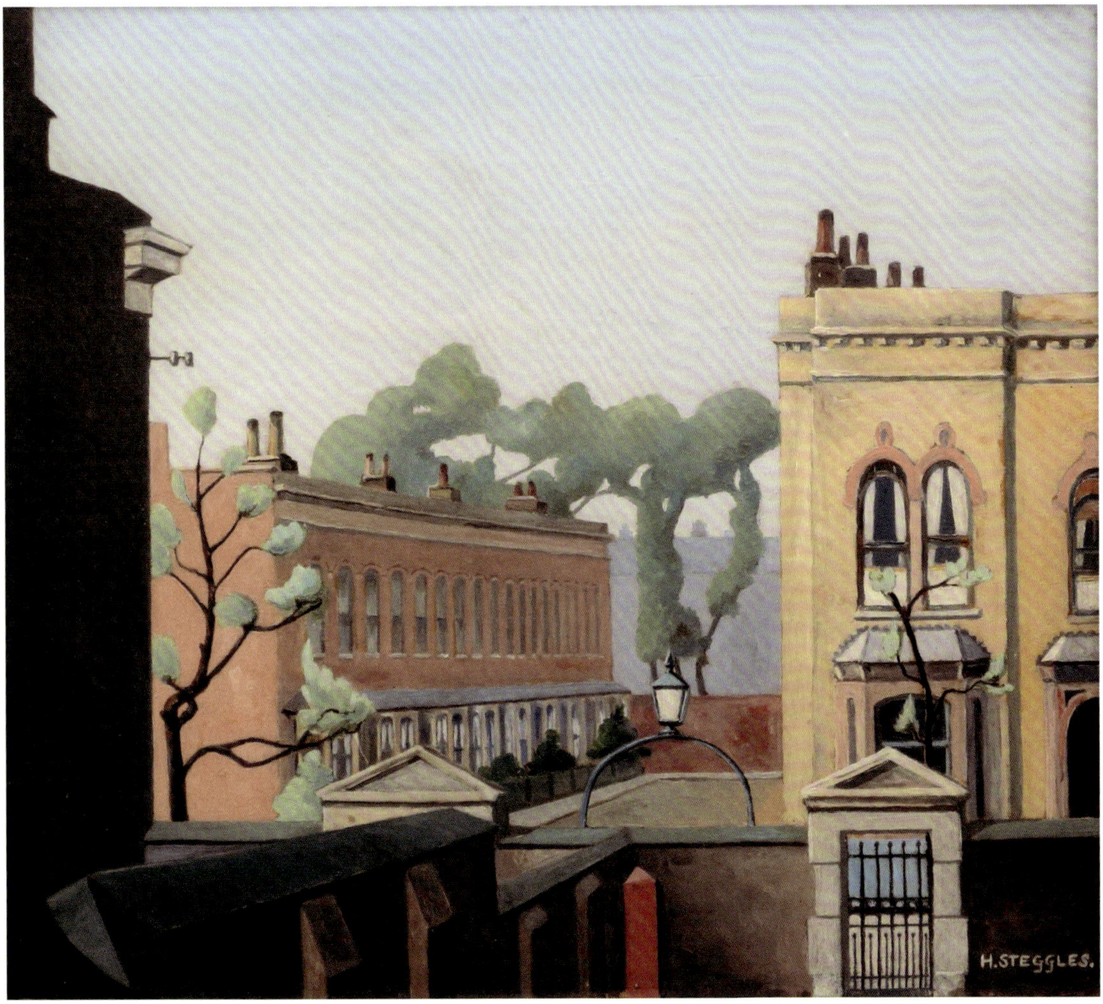

Grove Road, Bow, Harold Steggles (undated)

The precise location along Grove Road for this painting is uncertain. Also, being undated, it is difficult to assess dating accurately but, judging by Harold's style in other work, a date of c.1931/32 seems most likely.

Afternoon Light, Antill Road

Artist: Marc Gooderham

Medium: Acrylic on wood panel

Dimensions: 60 x 60cm

Date: 2024

To paint the East End is to paint the heart and soul of London. Having lived in both Bethnal Green and Hackney for many years, I share the East London Group's philosophy of capturing your surroundings and observing beauty in the everyday. Elwin Hawthorne's painting *Mile End Road* (1930) demonstrates this perfectly. The dramatic contrast of light and dark creates almost a monochrome effect. There is a harmonious interplay of street furniture and figures, and a sense of foreboding, which I love.

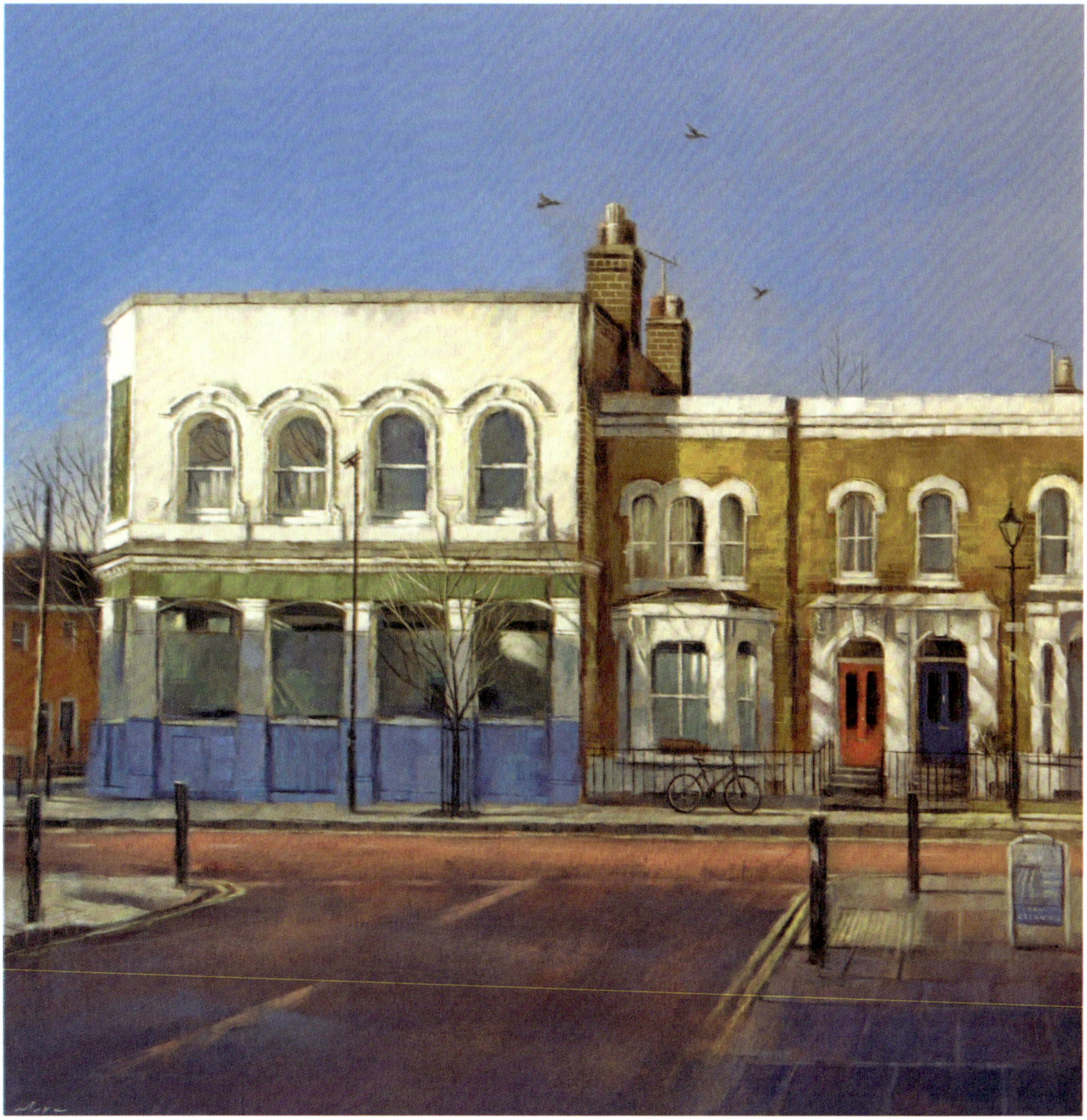

My creative process involves the exploration and sketching of the streets. I found myself returning to the terraced houses on Antill Road, a peaceful street nestled in the backwaters of Bow. It was the arched windows of the Duke of York that caught my eye – no longer the neighbourhood pub, but now residential dwellings; a transition I've always found intriguing. As the buildings basked in the afternoon light, I wanted to capture this moment of peace and tranquillity.

I've followed the Group's work closely since the release of David Buckman's publication, *From Bow to Biennale*. I also had the honour of participating in the recent Sky Arts documentary, *Brothers in Art: Walter and Harold Steggles*.

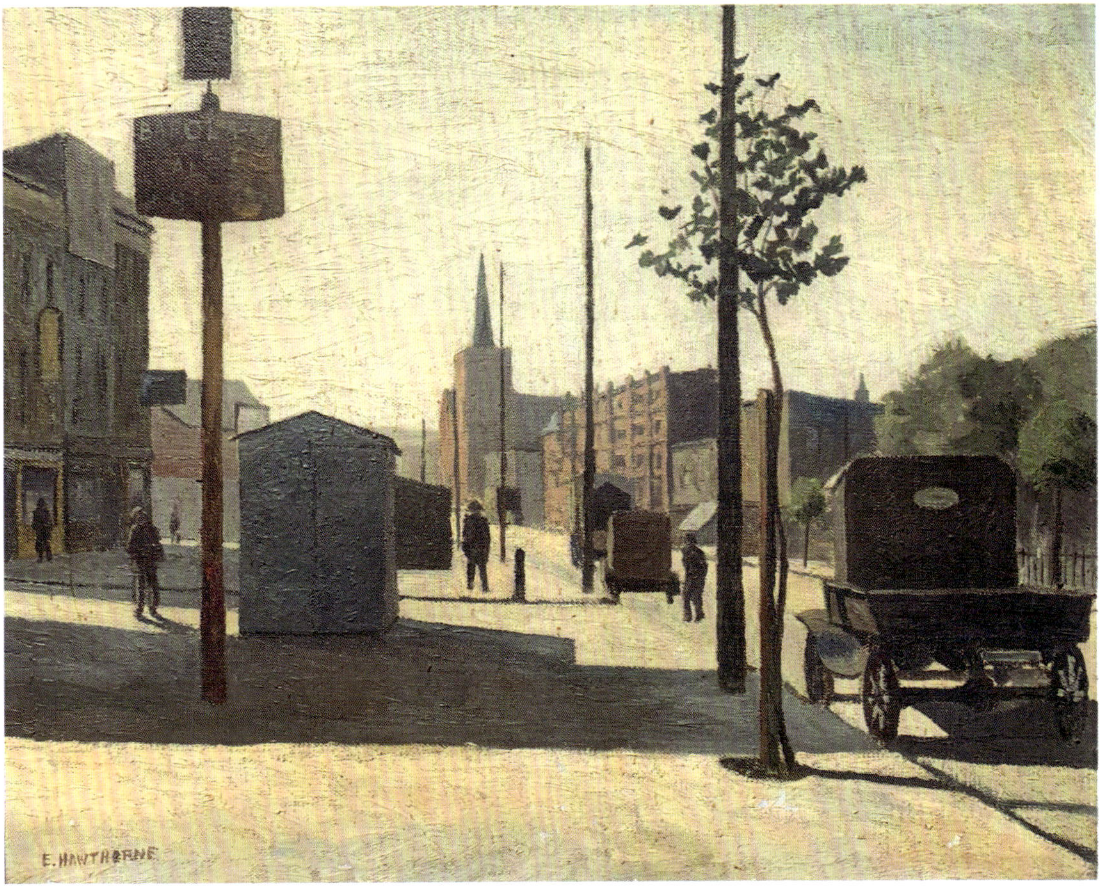

Mile End Road, Elwin Hawthorne (1930)

This was painted from a point adjacent to the Plough pub at 606 Mile End Road. A photo of the scene from Elwin's archives show that the pub sold Barclays beers. The Guardian Angels Church in the background also featured in at least one other piece of Elwin's work.

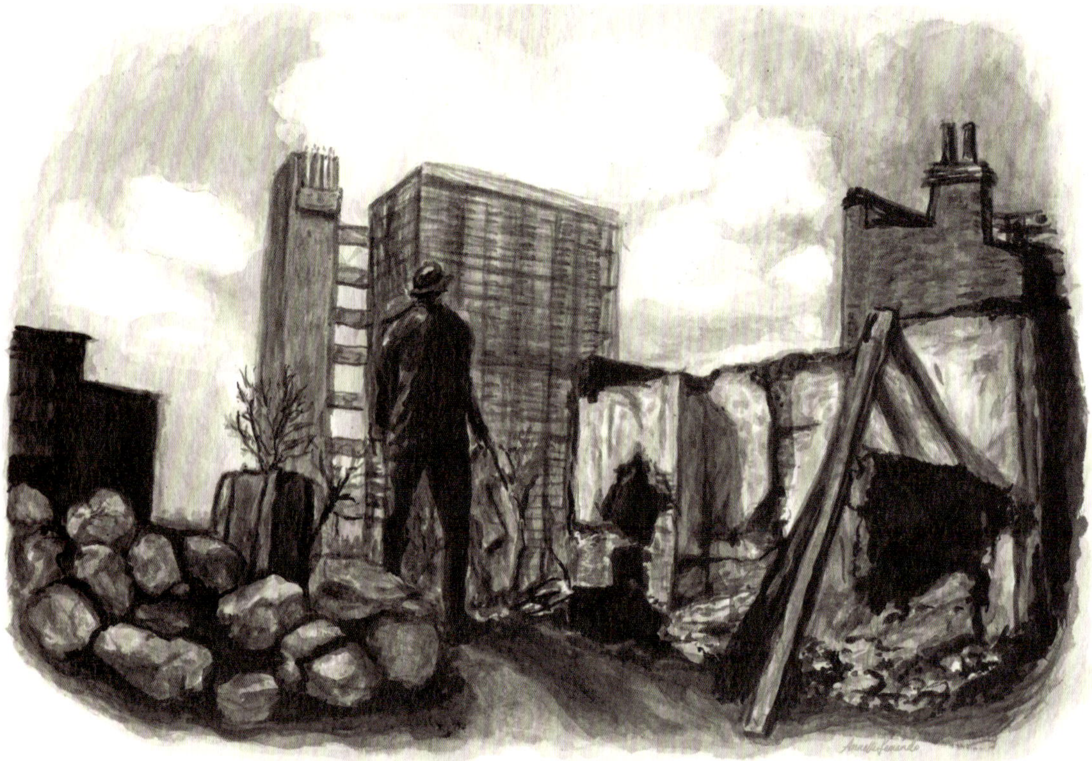

19

Sparrows Can't Sing

Artist: Annette Fernando

Medium: Ink on paper

Dimensions: 60 × 40cm

Date: 2024

My creative process begins with immersing myself in archival images and film reels, uncovering fragments of a bygone East London that persist in memory. Currently, I reside in a building marked for demolition, nestled between the commanding presence of the iconic Balfron Tower – a testament to Brutalist architecture – on one side, and the gleaming lights of Canary Wharf on the other. As I meander through the bustling streets of Bow, Mile End and Poplar, I'm continuously struck by the realization that this diverse and dynamic landscape is now my home. The urge to immortalize these scenes is fuelled by the knowledge that they, too, teeter on the edge of disappearance.

In my painting, I depict a scene from *Sparrows Can't Sing* (1963), a British film portraying the comedic and poignant struggles of working-class residents in the East End of London as they navigate love, life and the challenges of urban redevelopment. I chose the moment where Charlie, a returning sailor, discovers his demolished home in London's East End – a moment that resonates across time, inviting reflection on the cyclical nature of change and its impact on individuals and communities.

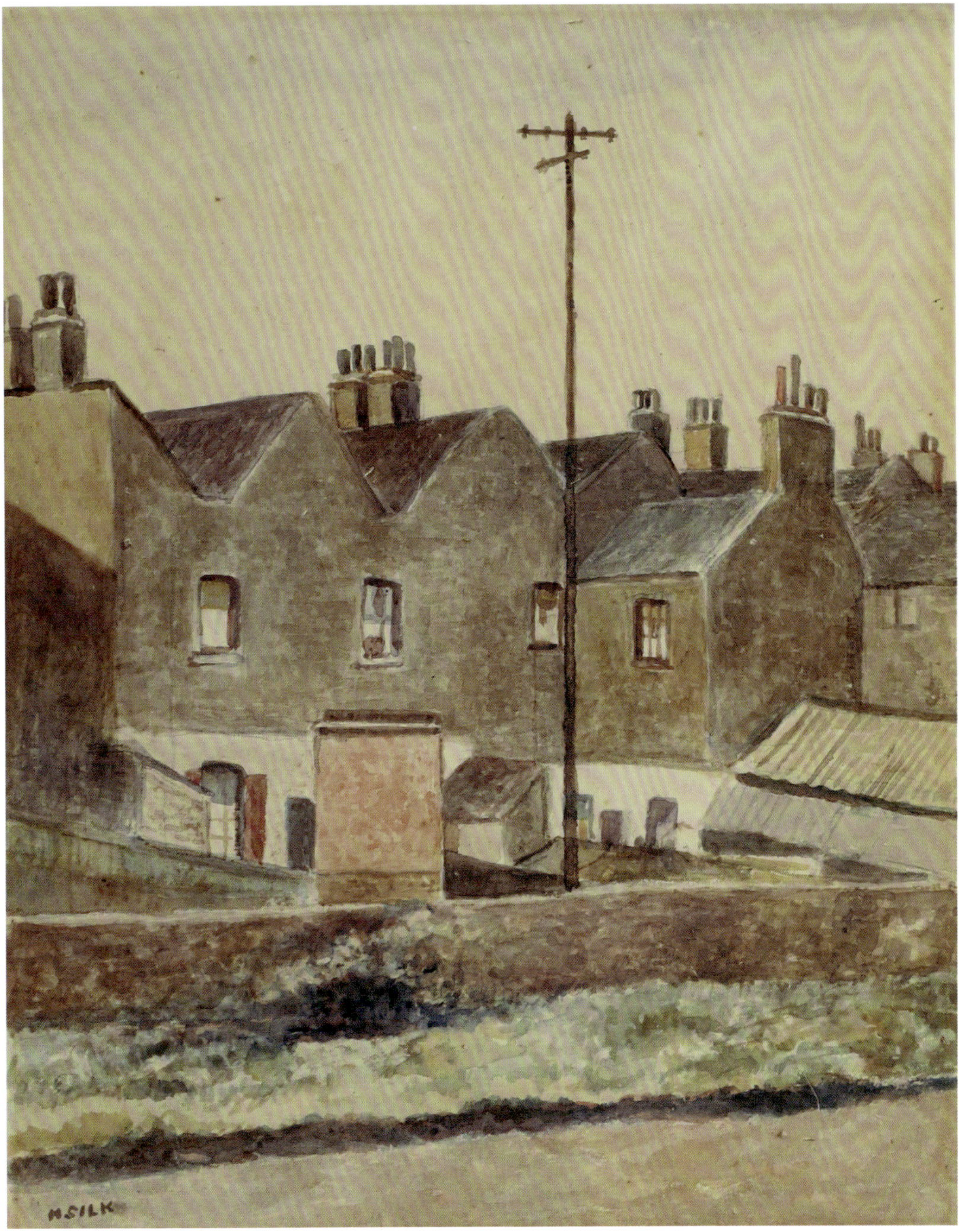

From an East End Window, Henry Silk (1931)

Henry Silk was a bachelor who rented a room from his sister, Ellen Hawthorne, who was Elwin Hawthorne's mother. The family lived at 11 Rounton Road in Bow and this painting depicts Henry's view from his bedroom window. A large proportion of his surviving work features still life work painted in his room, along with numerous views from his window.

Clarissa House (Poplar)

Artist: Harriet Mena Hill

Medium: Acrylic on salvaged ply panel

Dimensions: 41.5 × 57cm

Date: 2023/24

I was on my way to somewhere else when I passed Clarissa House in Poplar. It settled into my subconscious but kept coming back into view. As with all the places I paint, I spent a long time thinking about what was so compelling about it. I returned over several months to look at and absorb the place, listening for echoes of the former inhabitants in the deserted building.

It is so easy to dismiss places, neighbourhoods, housing estates and, in turn, whole communities through casual looking. This is what drew me to the work of

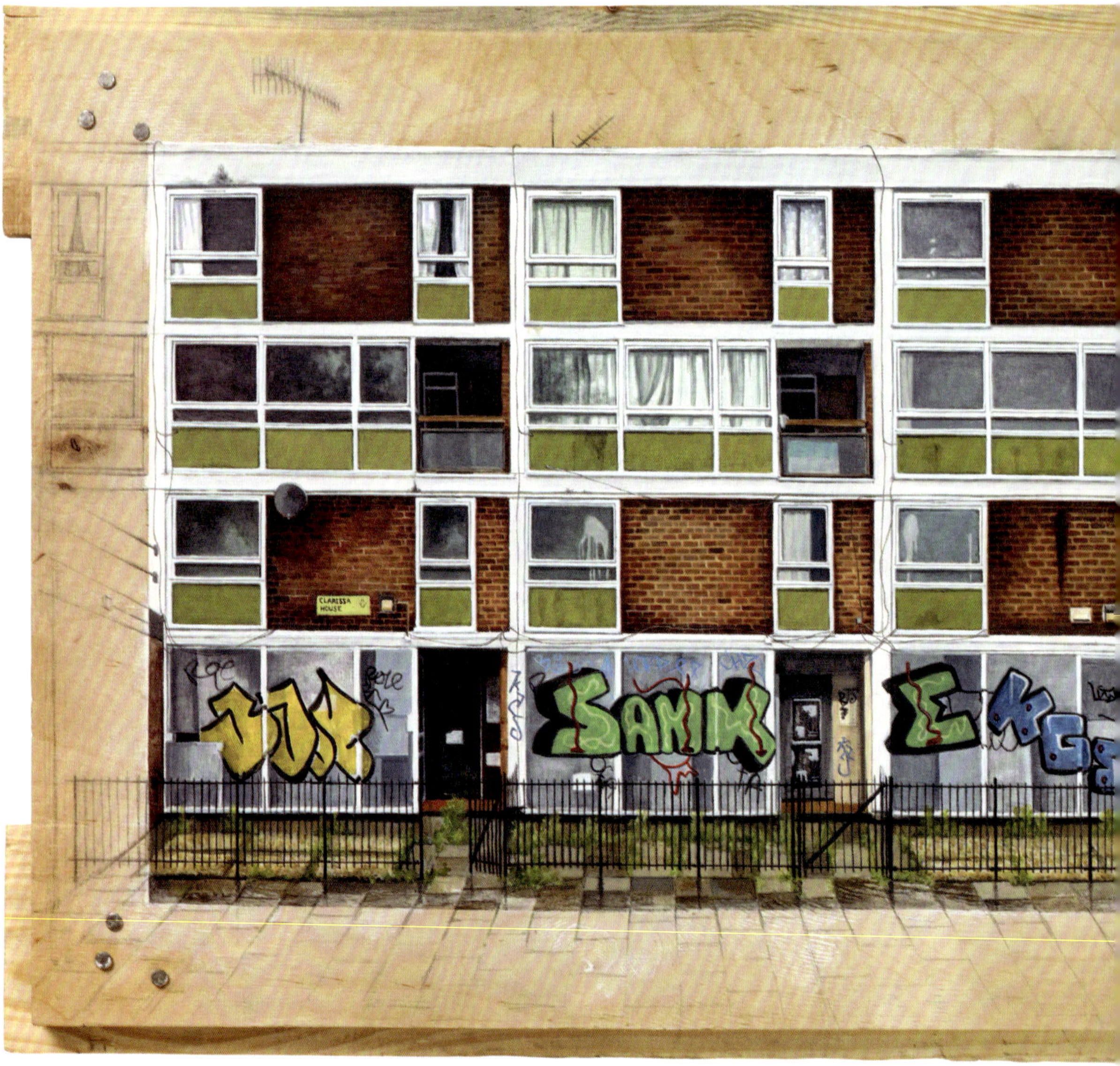

the East London Group: the close looking and the re-seeing of their environs not as harsh urban spaces but as familiar, tranquil places; places of living and community.

Clarissa House was an arresting place: compact, with a satisfying symmetry, individuated by possessions and curtains, disrupted by colourful graffiti and silvery metal hoardings. It spoke simultaneously of past histories and an uncertain future.

Clarissa House has now been demolished as part of the Chrisp Street Market Redevelopment Plan.

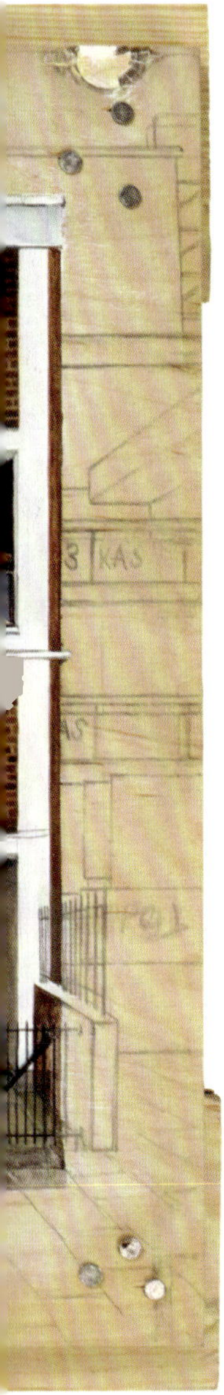

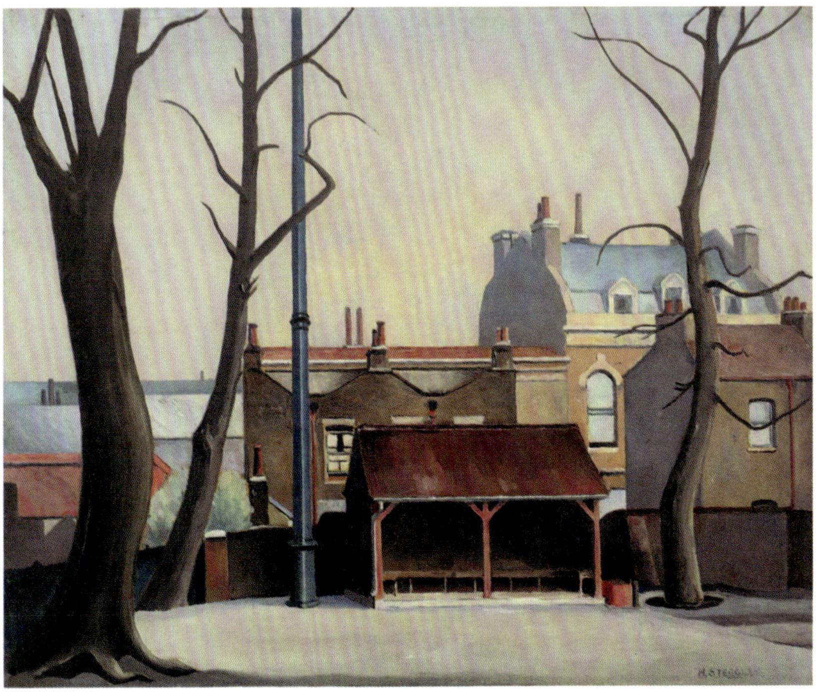

Grove Hall Park, Bow, Harold Steggles (1933)
Harold Steggles exhibited two paintings with very similar titles; the earlier one, of a different view, was shown in 1931. The large building in the background with the blue roof was the Five Bells Wharf pub at what was then 535 Old Ford Road.

21

Tower – Bryant and May Building

Artist: Gethin Evans

Medium: Oil on linen

Dimensions: 60 x 55cm

Date: 2023

I viewed the old Bryant and May building on a bright late summer afternoon and was immediately struck by how the light illuminated the imposing old water tower at the back of the building. The tower itself reminded me of some of the tower forms in Ambrogio Lorenzetti's *Unjust City* fresco in the Palazzo Pubblico, Siena. Initially, I wanted to capture the sense of a sunny afternoon and made a number of thumbnail colour studies from photographs I had taken. I then researched the history of the building, particularly the history of the match girls' strike of 1888.

The women's appalling working conditions often resulted in jaw disfigurement from the poisonous phosphorus used in the manufacture of the matches. This altered my 'vision' of the original image: the tower became some kind of witness, in my mind, to the building's former 'life'.

A small monochrome study enabled me to get closer to what I wanted. However, in the final painting, the harsh light illuminating the colour of the tower and the buildings, caught in the moment before a storm, seemed to capture the mood I was after.

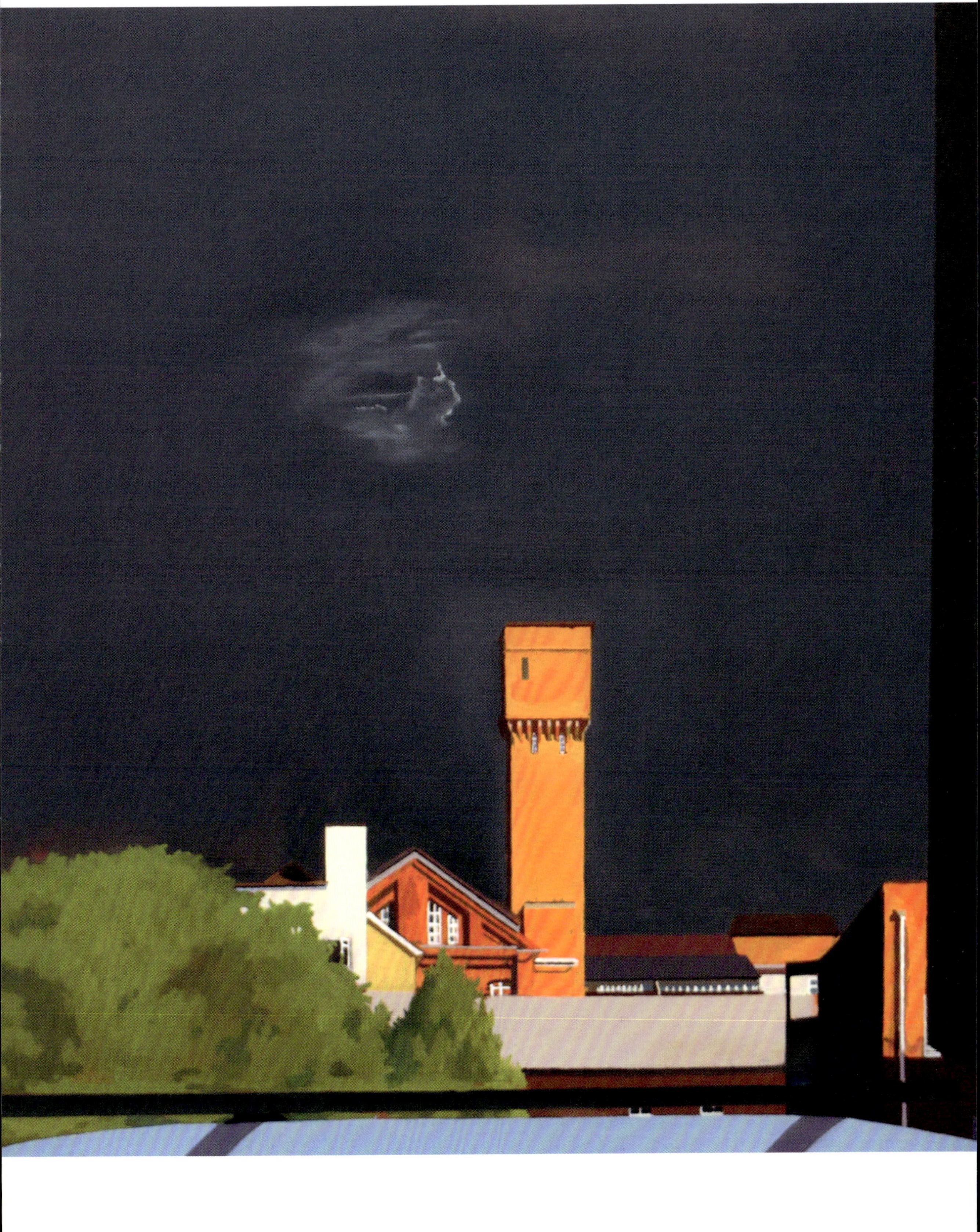

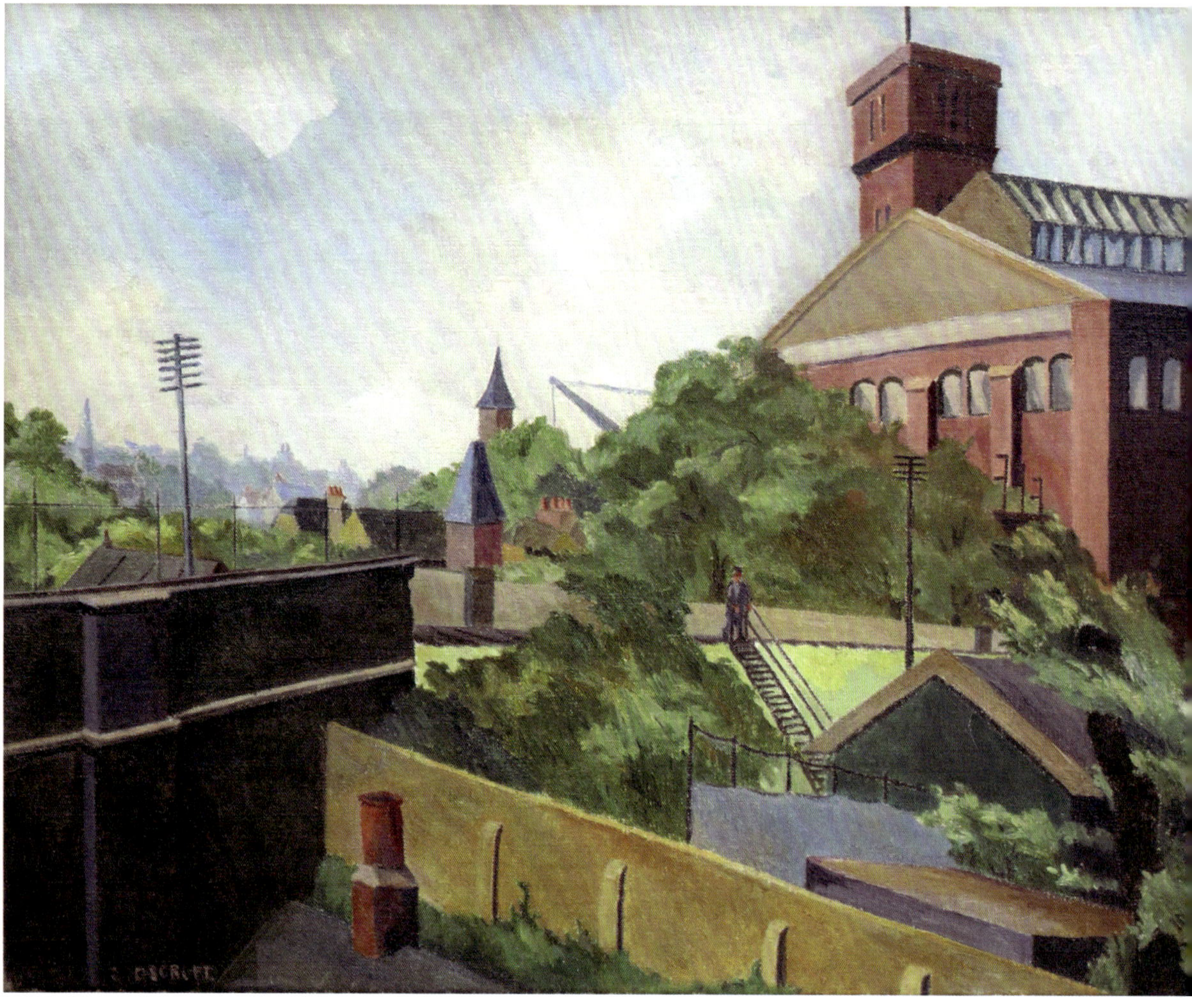

Bryant and May's, Grace Oscroft (undated)

Grace Oscroft's family had a house on Fairfield Road in Bow, not far from the Bryant and May factory, so it is very likely that this was a view that she painted from her window. The majority of Grace's work was within walking distance of the family's business premises at 212 Bow Road.

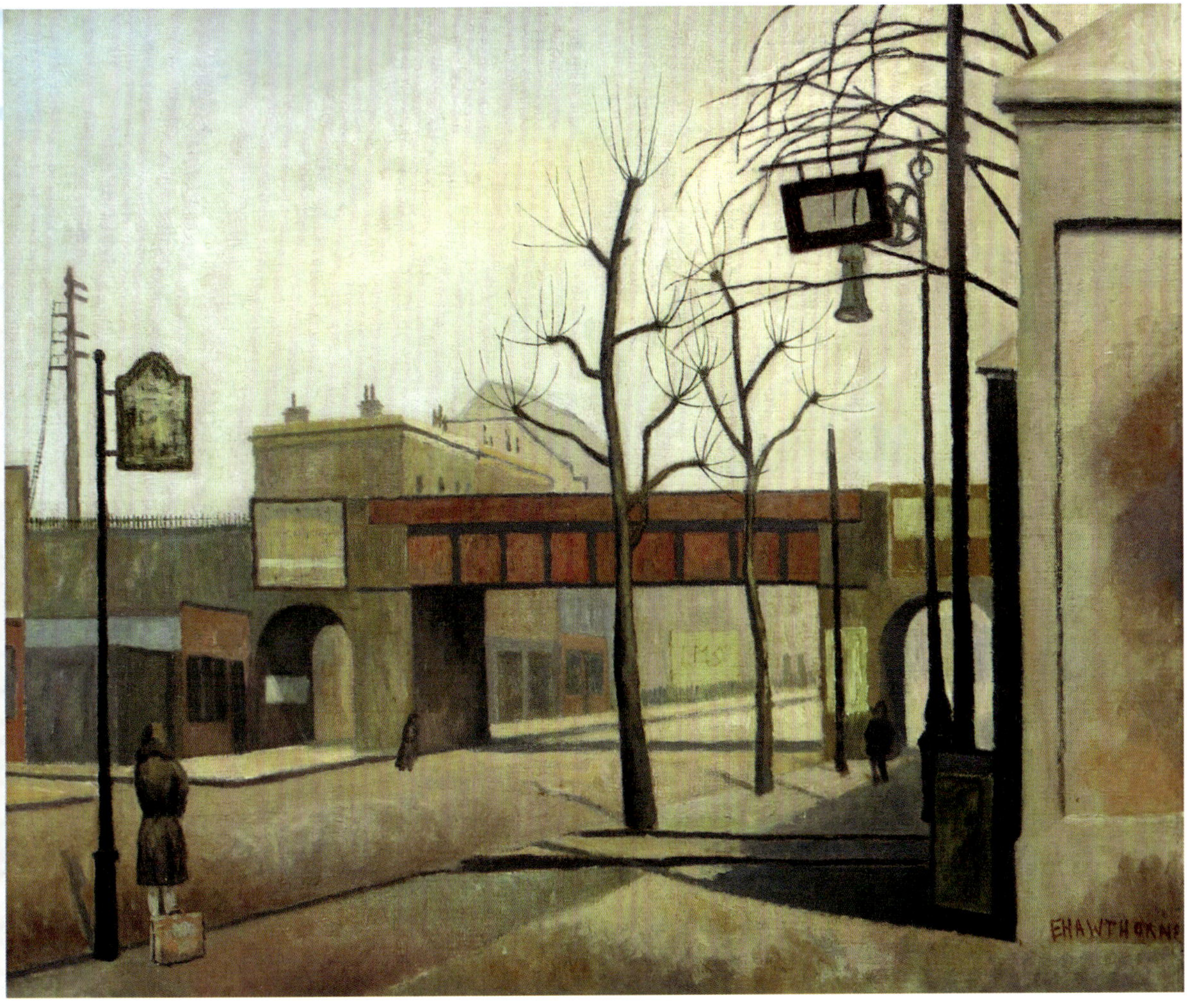

Bow Road, Elwin Hawthorne (1932)

First exhibited as *Bow*, this painting is described in the artist's notes as follows: 'From District station, looking East. Railway arch: stark trees. Bus sign on left with figure: bag on ground. Presented to W J Steggles.' By exchange, Walter Steggles gifted Elwin *Essex Farm*. Interestingly, neither painting appears in the Group's exhibition catalogues.

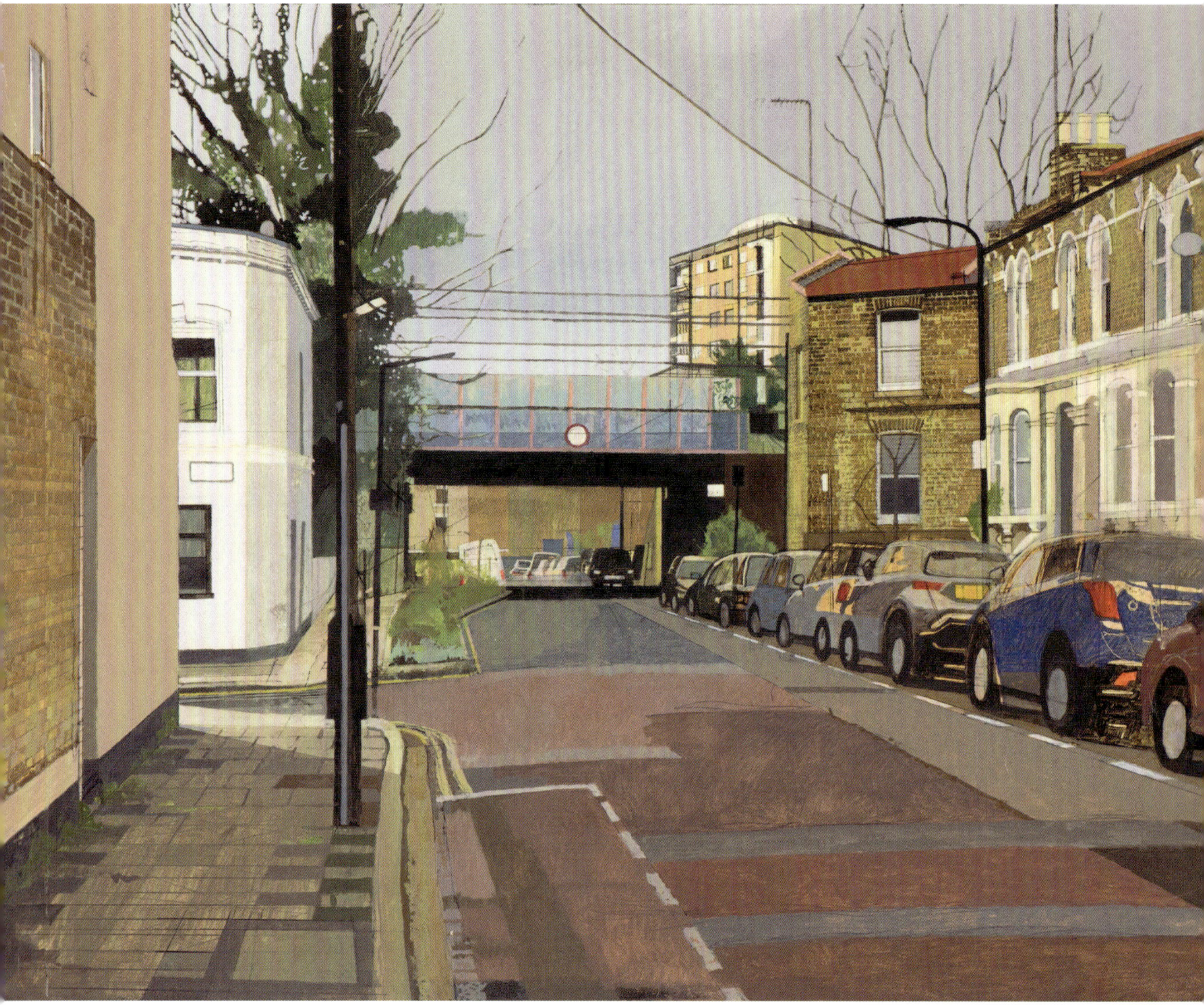

22

Blue Bridge, Wilton Way, Hackney

Artist: James Mackinnon
Medium: Oil on board
Dimensions: 40.5 × 52.5cm
Date: 2024

The railway bridge is a common and overlooked feature of the East London landscape. Railway lines and overhead electric wires cut through the urban landscape, functional and unassuming. The motif of the railway bridge appears in many of the East London Group's paintings – Elwin Hawthorne's *Bow Road* (1932) being of particular note.

Decades ago, I lived close to this bridge near London Fields, a short walk from the vibrant pubs, canals, tower blocks and open spaces that capture my imagination and often feature in my paintings. This simple pale blue bridge always held a magic for me that I wanted to capture.

The initial catalyst for my tackling this scene may have been John Minton's painting *Street and Railway Bridge*, which has been lodged in my memory for years. But where Minton's bridge inhabits the dramatic scene of a bomb-damaged London street, I wanted to turn the viewer's main focus onto this very ordinary but beautiful structure, sitting there quietly and unnoticed on an unremarkable working day. The challenge was how to place the bridge within the structures of a typical Hackney neighbourhood – the mixture of Victorian housing, lampposts and tower blocks – and allow it to take centre stage.

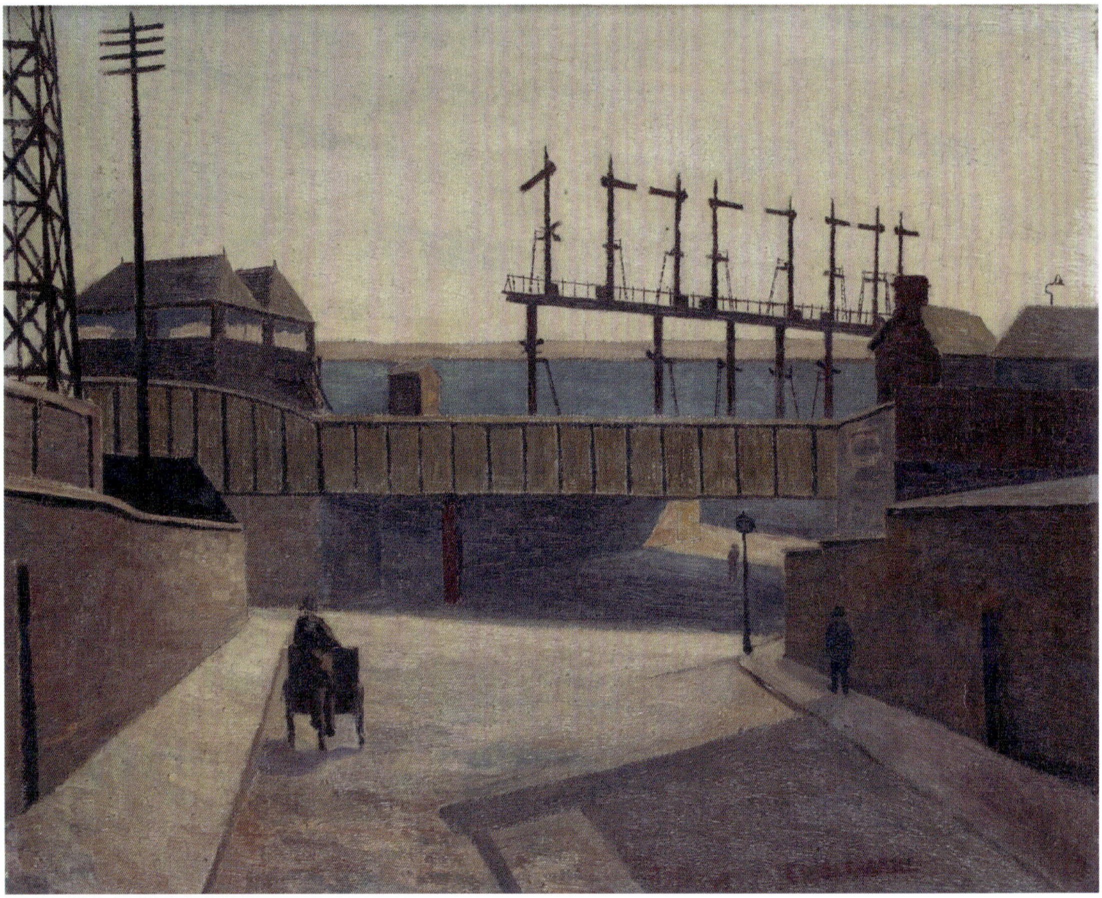

St Pancras Signals, Elwin Hawthorne (1930)

Several Group members depicted railway bridges in their work, but this is one of only a couple of known surviving paintings that show railway signals. According to his painting notes, Elwin would have taken his view from what was then known as Goods Way. The signal gantry and signal box are clearly marked on large-scale maps of the period. Elwin also painted nearby at Cumberland Market, Paddington Basin, Little Venice and Cumberland Basin.

Artist biographies

Beale, Philippa

www.philippabeale.com

Born Winchester, England, 1946. PG Dip Digital Image Making (Distinction), University of the Arts, 2007. Elected Fellow in Fine Art of the ITLHE for the UAL, 2006. PhD Research Degree Supervision, UAL, 2004. MCIM Chartered Institute of Business and Management, Kensington and Chelsea, 2002. MA Fine Art, Goldsmith's College, 1987. PG Dip Psychology and Philosophy, University of Reading, 1971. BA (Hons) Goldsmith's College, University of London, 1965. Winchester School of Art, 1962.

Elected President of the London Group in 1995 and Founding Member of the Arborealists in 2016. Solo exhibitions include: the Margate Gallery, 2023; Musée de Brux Vienne, France, 2022; Bermondsey Project Space, London, 2020; Chelsea Arts Club, London, 2018; Retrospective Conceptual Art Practice, LCC Galleries, London, 2007; Visions, Key London Ltd, 2001; From Wilson to Callaghan, video viewing, ICA, 1997; Musée des Dortoirs des Moines, St Benoit, Poitiers, France, 1988; Southampton City Art Gallery, 1984; 'Baby Love', Angela Flowers Gallery, London, 1982; Akumulatory 2 Galleria, Poznan, Poland, 1982; Richard Demarco Gallery, Edinburgh, 1977; 'Collected from There', Angela Flowers Gallery, and 'Collected from Here', Acme Gallery, London, 1978; Park Square Gallery, Leeds, 1976; Camden Arts Centre, London, 1972. Collections include: Tate Britain, ACGB, Southampton City Art Gallery, Bourg de Brux France, Kraków Museum of Modern Art and Camden Borough Council.

Blum, Alexandra

www.alexblum.co.uk

Alexandra Blum's work has been exhibited at the Museum of the Home (permanent collection acquisition), Hackney Museum and London Transport Museum, among many other venues. Solo shows include 'Wayfaring', Fitzrovia Gallery, London, 2023 (catalogue essay by Dr Rachel Sloan, Associate Curator for Works on Paper, the Courtauld Gallery). Awards include the Hugh Casson Drawing Prize, 2019, the Oppenheim-John Downes Memorial Trust Award, 2012, and the David Gluck Memorial Bursary for Drawing, 2008 (first prize). She was artist-in-residence at Dalston Square construction site (2008–10) and was awarded a post-graduate MEXT research scholarship in painting at Kyoto City University of Arts, Japan (1996–98).

Craven, Tim

Tim Craven was born in Birmingham and trained in fine art at Stourbridge College of Art (BA degree, 1976) before completing a Postgraduate Diploma in the Conservation of Easel Paintings at Gateshead Technical College in 1979. He was employed at Southampton City Art Gallery from 1980 until 2017 in Conservation, Collection Management and as Curator. In 2013, he founded the Arborealists artists' collective (thirty-eight exhibitions and nine publications to date), and was elected a member of the London Group in 2015. He became Chair of the Friends of Southampton's Museums, Archives and Galleries in 2019 and joined the board of the British Association of Friends of Museums in 2021. In 2022, he formed the Southern Exhibitions Group, which initiates and delivers diverse fine art exhibitions in different venues, and he regularly lectures on art and history subjects. His work is held in the New Art Gallery, Walsall; Nature in Art Gallery, Gloucester; and the Longleat Wessex collection, as well as in private collections worldwide.

Evans, Gethin

www.gethinevans.com

Gethin Evans was born in Maesteg, South Wales, and has a studio in the East End of London. He studied Fine Art Painting at Camberwell School of Arts and Crafts and Postgraduate at the Slade School of Fine Art. He has exhibited widely in group shows, including Threadneedle Prize, ING Discerning Eye, Royal Academy Summer exhibitions and Street Road Artists Space, Pennsylvania, USA. He was co-founder of the Foundation

Course at Trinity Buoy Wharf and has been a visiting tutor to the New York Studio School. He exhibits regularly with Tregony Gallery in Cornwall and has paintings in various private collections.

Fernando, Annette

www.annettefernando.carbonmade.com

Annette Fernando, born in London, UK, in 1991, holds a BA in Fine Art from Central Saint Martins and received the Cultural Leaders Postgraduate Scholarship from Sotheby's Institute of Art. She has exhibited extensively in solo and group shows across the UK, France, Spain, Sri Lanka and Hong Kong. She won the Jerwood Drawing Prize in 2014 and was selected for the Royal Academy Summer Exhibition in 2021 and 2023. Her work is in private collections in the USA, France, Hong Kong and the UK. In addition to her artistic practice, Annette is a curator and writer in the arts.

Fletcher, Doreen

www.doreenfletcherartist.com

'My focus as a painter lies in absorbing the memory of familiar places over time, recording the traces left by humans on the environment to create a visual story that I can share with the viewer.

'I have always been committed to drawing and painting what might be termed "the almost gone" or the "forgotten pockets of life" that constitute my immediate external environment. I search for an outcome that is emotionally evocative and that also works structurally as a formal composition.'

Gooderham, Marc

www.marcgooderham.co.uk

Marc Gooderham's paintings focus on the unique architecture of city life. He finds an attractive melancholy in street corners and the crumbling grandeur of old shop fronts, capturing scenes that hold an almost cinematic quality.

Marc's paintings evoke the sense of loneliness that is inherent in any large city. But the stillness of his work also invites contemplation – of the lives once lived here and the new lives that continue. He is a member of the Society of Graphic Fine Art; founded in 1919, it is recognized as the only foundation in the UK dedicated to drawing. Marc Gooderham's work is held in both private and overseas collections.

Hepher, David

www.flowersgallery.com/artists/30-david-hepher/
Instagram @flowersgallery

David Hepher was born in 1935. Between the ages of six and nine, he was afflicted with tuberculosis and was consequently relatively isolated, which gave him time to draw and paint. Later his housemaster at school, an émigré German painter, encouraged him to continue with his painting. Coupled with his parents' close friendship with Eric Ravilious and his interest in landscape and architectural subjects, he was drawn to attend both Camberwell Art School and the Slade, both heavily influenced by the Euston Road School. In 1971 he was taken on by the Angela Flowers Gallery and has been represented by them ever since. He has supported his painting by teaching part-time in art schools, principally at Camberwell, Chelsea and the Slade. He has exhibited both nationally and internationally on many occasions and is represented in countless public and private collections.

Hyman, Timothy, R.A.

www.timothyhyman.net

Timothy Hyman was born in 1946 and was brought up in London. He studied painting at the Slade, 1963–7. He has had ten solo London exhibitions, and his works are held in many public collections. Hyman was elected as painter/Royal Academician in 2011. He is the author of *Bonnard* (1998), *Sienese Painting* (2003, 2022) and *The World New Made* (2016, 2022), all published by Thames & Hudson. Hyman curated 'Narrative Paintings' (Arnolfini/ICA 1979) and 'Stanley Spencer', Tate (2000). He is a visiting professor at Baroda, India, and wrote a pioneering monograph on Bhupen Khakhar in 1997.

Johnson, Ben

www.benjohnsonartist.com

Ben Johnson studied at the Royal College of Art and lives and works in London. He is best known for his paintings based on architectural spaces and his large-scale cityscapes, which include panoramas of Hong Kong, Zürich, Jerusalem, Liverpool and London, which was completed as part of a residency at the National Gallery, London, in 2010.

Johnson has exhibited widely in galleries and museums across the world, including the Institute of Contemporary Arts, London; the Walker Art Gallery, Liverpool; the Art Institute of Chicago; Kunsthalle Tübingen; and the Museo Thyssen-Bornemisza, Madrid. A retrospective of his paintings was exhibited at the Southampton City Museum and Art Gallery in 2015.

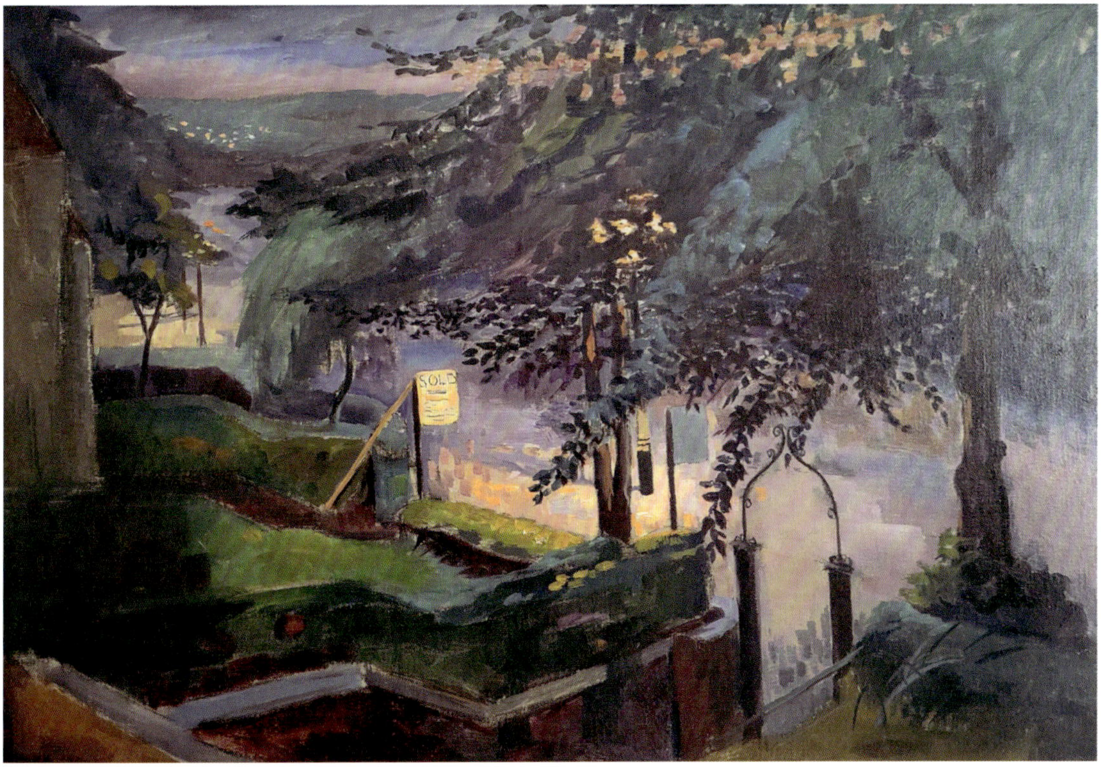

A View from 46 Platt's Lane, Hampstead, Phyllis Bray (undated)

Phyllis Bray lived at 46 Platt's Lane in Hampstead for many years, so this is a view that she would have known intimately. Her exhibition listings from the Group's active period from 1929 to 1936 indicate that the majority of her work at that time featured landscapes, seascapes or still life images, with only a very few 'urban' images. None of Phyllis's 'urban' images are known to survive, so this is a rare example of her work in that genre.

He has undertaken commissions for the Royal Institute of British Architects, the British Museum and National Museums Liverpool, as well as for IBM, HSBC, JP Morgan, British Steel and Hong Kong Telecommunications, among others. His work is included in permanent collections worldwide, including the Victoria and Albert Museum, London; the Centre Georges Pompidou, Paris; the Museum of Modern Art, New York; the Regional Services Museum, Hong Kong; and the Government Art Collection.

Johnson, Michael

Michael Johnson took a first in Fine Art at Reading University and was awarded a Postgraduate Scholarship at the Byam Shaw School of Art. He has been painting for fifty years, exhibiting widely in solo and group shows. He showed in the USA for the first time in the autumn of 2024. Michael has been shortlisted for the Ruskin Prize, Marmite Prize, Threadneedle Prize, Lynn Painter Stainers Prize, the London Group Biennial, the Derwent Prize and the Discerning Eye, and is a regular exhibitor at the Royal Academy Summer exhibition. He was a double prize winner at the Royal Scottish Academy Annual in 2023. He has a painting in the Museum of London collection.

Lowe, Sarah
www.sarahloweart.com

Born in 1965, Sarah Lowe studied Fine Art at Reading University. She has lived in East London for most of her life and paints scenes from the city and suburbs around her. Her work reflects on the constant changes of city life and the conflicting emotions of detachment and intimacy that city dwellers have, both with one another and with their urban surroundings.

Mackinnon, James
www.jamesmackinnonfineart.com

James Mackinnon (born 1968) showed an early interest in drawing buildings, in particular the Post Office Tower! Aged eleven, he won an art scholarship to Dulwich College. After completing a foundation course at Saint Martins, he graduated with honours from Kingston Polytechnic. He initially worked in set design, before becoming a full-time painter. He was supported by the Millinery Works Gallery for many years. It was with their encouragement that he had a solo show, 'From Hackney to Hastings', in 2017. David Buckman, author of *From Bow to Biennale: Artists of the East London Group*, describes Mackinnon's work thus: 'he magically transforms the commonplace, producing pictures suffused with an air of mystery'. The Museum of London holds Mackinnon's *London Fields East – The Ghetto*, made in collaboration with photographer Tom Hunter.

McIntyre, Fiona

www.fionamcintyre.com

Fiona McIntyre was born in Nairobi, Kenya, in 1963. She has a BA from Edinburgh College of Art, an MA from Winchester School of Art (in Barcelona), and was mentored in Sweden by surrealist Master Printmaker Bertil Lundberg at Grafikskolan Forum Malmö. Fiona has exhibited in more than forty exhibitions, including 'Under The Greenwood: Picturing The British Tree' at Lymington Museum and Art Gallery, and 'The Romantic Thread In British Art' at Southampton City Art Gallery. She conducted a residency at the Sidney Nolan Trust, leading to a solo exhibition, 'Dreaming The Land', then a Residency at Hosking Houses Trust on the banks of the River Stour. Fiona is a founding member of the Arborealists, and an elected member of the Royal Society of Painter-Printmakers. Her work is in public collections including the Ashmolean, Oxford, and Bohuslän Konstmuseum, Sweden.

Mena Hill, Harriet

www.harrietmenahill.com

Instagram @harrietmena_hill

Harriet Mena Hill was born in 1966 in Paddington, London. She studied Painting and Printmaking at Camberwell School of Art & Crafts in 1984–89 and took a studio directly from college, having been offered a solo exhibition at her degree show. She has exhibited regularly over the past thirty-five years in solo exhibitions at the Eagle Gallery, the Fine Art Society and the Ingleby Gallery, among others, and in group exhibitions in the UK and internationally.

Alongside her painting practice she has been shortlisted numerous times in both the Trinity Buoy Wharf and Derwent Drawing Prizes.

She has work in many public and private collections, including the Government Art Collection, the Museum of London, the Whitaker Museum, St John's College, Oxford, the Fleming Wyfold Art Foundation and Murray Edwards (New Hall), Cambridge. She was a gallery artist at the National Gallery in London for eleven years. She continues her museum education work at the Foundling Museum in combination with her community engagement projects on the Aylesbury Estate in southeast London.

Pemberton, Alex

www.alexanderpemberton.blogspot.com/

After graduating from Chelsea School of Art in 1981, Alexander Pemberton won a British Council Award to work in Spain. In 1983–4, he won an Elizabeth Greenshields Award to paint in Mexico. Recent solo exhibitions were held at Abbott & Holder: 'Thames Paintings' (2014) and 'Still Lifes' (2022). In 2009–10, he showed paintings of the Thames at the River & Rowing Museum, Henley.

In 2002–5, he worked with the Embrace the Middle East charity to make exhibitions based on his journeys to Israel/Palestine and Armenia. Previously, he had solo exhibitions at Cadogan Contemporary (1992) and Chappel Galleries (2006), and has exhibited in many group shows. He has paintings in many private collections.

Poh, Nicole

www.nicolepoh.com

Nicole Poh (b. 2000, Hong Kong) is an artist based in London. She graduated from Camberwell College of Arts in 2023 with a BA in Fine Art Painting and has recently graduated from the Royal College of Art with an MA in Painting. She has participated in various group shows in London.

Rosen, Hilary

www.hilaryrosen.co.uk

Hilary Rosen was born and bred in London. Her maternal grandparents lived in Cable Street in the East End and her aunts lived in Bethnal Green, so she spent a lot of her childhood in these urban areas. She took her BA in Nottingham, and her MA in London at the Royal College of Art. Most of her work concerns the urban environment. Some of her solo shows have been at Galerie Hilde Leiss, Hamburg, Boundary Gallery and the Royal National Theatre. She has work in both private and public collections, including the Museum of London, Zeiss Collection, Hamburg LV, Prasad Hyderabad, India, St Mary's Hospital, London, and UCH, London.

Scott-Miller, Melissa

www.scottmillerart.com

Melissa Scott-Miller studied at the Slade School of Fine Art in 1977–81. She has received numerous awards, including the Lynn Painter Stainers award first prize in 2008, and the grand prize at the Royal Society of British Artists in 2024. She is a member of the Royal Society of Portrait Painters and the New English Art Club. Melissa has had many solo and group shows. In 2023 she had a solo exhibition at Chris Beetles Gallery. She can often be spotted painting around London. She teaches at the Royal Drawing School and Heatherley School of Fine Art.

Watson, Grant

www.grantwatson.co.uk

Grant Watson is a London-based painter. He studied Fine Art at Portsmouth Polytechnic in 1985–88 and Eastern Illinois University in 1988–90. In 1993 and 1994 he studied under Karel Appel and Eric Fischl at the Antonio Ratti Foundation in Italy, where he won a purchase prize for drawing. He has exhibited widely. Notable shows include the Creekside Open, Beep Painting Prize, Wells Art Contemporary, the Discerning Eye, the New Gallery Walsall, and the Royal Academy Summer exhibition. He was awarded the Doreen McIntosh prize at the New English Art Club annual. In 2023, Grant was elected member of the New English Art Club.

About the curators

Creber, Frank

www.frankcreber.space/

Frank Creber, recipient of the national Barclays Bank Young Painters award in 1986, draws on extensive topographical cityscape sketches in East London, reflecting its evolution since the 1990s. As both an artist and a project manager at the renowned Bromley by Bow Centre, he intertwines memory and observation in his paintings, narrating the stories of local families. His work is in public and private collections including the Royal Collection, Clarence House, and the Mother and Children's Unit, Mildmay Mission Hospital.

Since 1992, Creber has curated acclaimed exhibitions at venues including the Southbank Centre, Barbican Concourse Gallery and Tobacco Dock London. Notable shows include 'Walking on Water', a mile-long exhibition at ExCel London, in partnership with Grand Designs, organized by Water City CIC, for which he is artistic director, curating exhibition stands with Emirates Airline, CASA at UCL, UEL, Barrett London, UCL Partners and Poplar Harca and a continuous display of 100 paintings by the artist. He co-founded the Urban Contemporaries Group with exhibitions at Espacio Gallery and Coningsby Gallery that foster a discourse on contemporary urban issues.

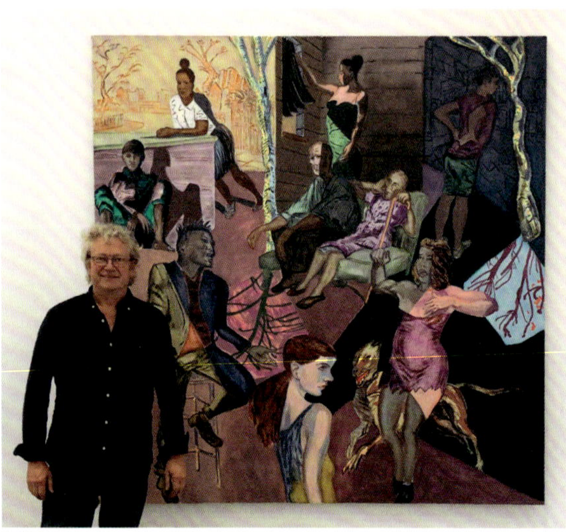

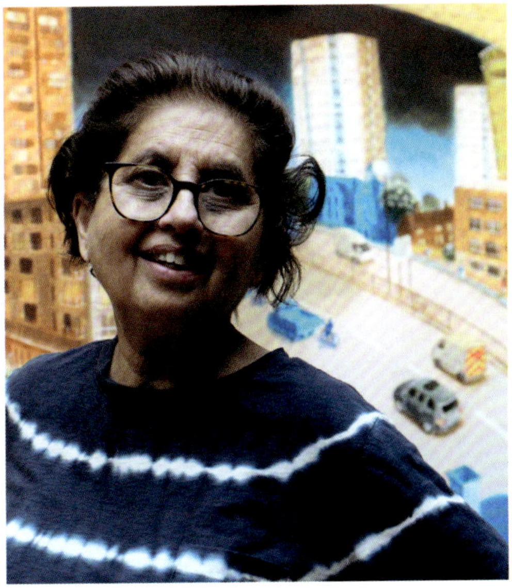

Farooqui, Ferha

www.ferhafarooqui.weebly.com

Ferha Farooqui was born in Hyderabad, India, and came to London in the late 1960s. She studied Fine Art at Winchester School of Art in the early 1980s under Gillian Ayres and Vanessa Jackson. Her work can be seen in the collections of the V&A Print Department, the Guildhall Art Gallery, and the London Borough of Newham Heritage Archives, as well as being held in private collections in Rome, Sydney and the UK.

She won a Dulwich Open Exhibition prize and her work has been shown at the Freud Museum, the V&A Museum of Childhood (now Young V&A), Pushkin House, the Barbican Library and the Whitechapel Open Exhibition, among others. In 2019, Ferha set up the Urban Contemporaries Group with Frank Creber, bringing together a group of painters with a shared interest in capturing the urban condition and offering themed exhibitions about encounters with the city at the Espacio Gallery, Coningsby Gallery and Lauderdale House. This came about because of her passion for promoting work that reflects diverse voices in the field of contemporary urban painting. The exhibition 'In the Footsteps of the East London Group' and its accompanying book forms an exciting development in this journey.

Waltham, Alan

www.eastlondongroup.co.uk

As a private individual with no formal background or training in the art world, Alan was pitched into this new environment in 2008/9 due to the inheritance of some of the works and archives of his wife's late uncle, Walter Steggles. Walter and his younger brother Harold had exhibited widely in the late 1920s and 1930s but, beyond that, Alan and his wife had no context as to their artistic achievements. While sorting through old catalogues and correspondence, it became clear just what they and the Group had achieved and, as time has gone on, Alan has become steeped in their world and that of the East London Group and has discovered the true scope of their achievements and reputation in their day. Alan has used various social media platforms to add immeasurably to that understanding, most notably Twitter.

Alan has launched three websites for the East London Group and runs profiles for the group on Facebook (@East London Group), Instagram (@eastlondongroup) and Twitter (@EastLndonGroup). He has been closely involved in seven ELG exhibitions in recent years, four of which he has curated, and with a fifth in prospect.

Acknowledgements

Ferha Farooqui and Frank Creber

We are very grateful to Alan Waltham for bringing together these original paintings by the East London Group; to Sophie Hill and the Nunnery Gallery team; and to Polly Powell, Nicola Newman and Bella Skertchly of Batsford Books for enthusiastically developing this idea with us. It has been a rewarding journey. We would also like to express our grateful thanks to Richard Hand for his insight and support in curating this exhibition.

Alan Waltham

I would like to place on record my thanks, and those of all ELG members' families, to David Buckman for having the tenacity to put together his book *From Bow to Biennale* (which took many years); to Clive Boutle, who had the vision to publish the book; to Rosamond Murdoch for seeing the potential in the Group's work; and to Sophie Hill for hosting this, our third exhibition at the Nunnery Gallery. Finally, we are all deeply indebted to Polly Powell and her team at Batsford Books for producing this catalogue.

Sophie Hill, Director of Arts & Events, Bow Arts

I would like to thank Ferha Farooqui and Frank Creber, the visionary curators of the Urban Contemporaries Group of artists, keeping the celebration of London alive through painting. We are forever indebted to Alan Waltham, without whom none of our exhibitions featuring the East London Group would have been possible. I would also like to thank all the lenders of the East London Group works, enabling them to once again come together. And, finally, to all the Nunnery Gallery team who give so much to every one of our exhibitions.

Picture credits

Page 31: © David Hepher, photography by Reinis Lismanis
Page 35: © Doreen Fletcher
Page 38–39: © BEN JOHNSON all rights reserved DACS. Collection of Plus One Gallery.
Page 40–41, 42: © Frank Creber
Page 44, 45: © Ferha Farooqui, photography by Richard Hand
Page 48: © Sarah Lowe
Page 52: © Michael Johnson, photography by David Quinn
Page 54, 55, 56: © Grant Watson, photography by Benjamin Deakin
Page 58–59: © Alex Pemberton, photography by Cole Pemberton
Page 62, 63: © Alexandra Blum, photography by John Howard Davies (www.johnhowarddavies.com)
Page 64, 65, 66: © Fiona McIntyre
Page 69: © Philippa Beale
Page 72–73: © Hilary Rosen, photography by Mathew Ward
Page 75: © Nicole Poh
Page 78: © Melissa Scott-Miller
Page 81: © Timothy Hyman
Page 82: © Tim Craven, photography by Alison Craven
Page 84: © Marc Gooderham
Page 86: © Annette Fernando
Page 88–89: © Harriet Mena Hill, photography by Kevin Dutton
Page 91: © Gethin Evans
Page 94: © James Mackinnon, photography by Tim Nathan (media25.org)
Page 96: © Camden Local Studies and Archives Centre
Page 106: Phil Ashcroft

Images of the East London Group's work kindly provided by Alan Waltham – pages 2, 8, 11, 14, 18, 22, 24–25, 28, 29, 32, 33, 36, 37, 43, 46, 47, 50, 51, 57, 60–61, 67, 70, 71, 76, 77, 79, 83, 85, 87, 89, 92, 93, 101.

About the Nunnery Gallery

Housed in a former nineteenth-century convent building, the Nunnery Gallery is Bow Arts' not-for-profit art space, surrounded by artists' studios. The exhibition programme pushes boundaries with an original and creative approach that explores the stories of East London and celebrates today's artistic talent.

Previous to 'In the Footsteps of the East London Group', the Gallery has presented two exhibitions featuring the East London Group. 'The East London Group of Artists: From Bow to Biennale c.1928–1936' (2014) was the first exhibition retrospective of the East London Group following a rekindling of interest in its artists after the release of David Buckman's book *From Bow to Biennale*. 'The Working Artist: The East London Group' (2017), curated by Michael Rosen and Emma-Louise Williams followed, with a focus on the work of ELG member Albert Turpin.

Other exhibitions with a particular focus on East London have included 'Doreen Fletcher: A Retrospective' (2019) and the National Lottery Heritage-funded exhibition series 'Raw Materials', which explores the industrial and social history of East London one material at a time.

Open to the public six days a week, all Nunnery Gallery exhibitions are free to enter. The Nunnery is part of educational arts charity Bow Arts Trust. Since 1994, Bow Arts have nurtured London's diverse creativity and talent, creating opportunities to work, learn and enjoy affordable, lifelong access to the arts.